Schaumburg Township District Library
130 South Roselle Road
Schaumburg, Illinois 60193

The
Farmstead
Egg
Cookbook

Terry Golson

Photographs by
Ben Fink

St. Martin's Press ❧ New York

Acknowledgments

Putting this book together has been so much fun. Thanks to my agent, Carla Glasser, who placed it in the hands of Elizabeth Beier. Not only is Elizabeth a wonderful editor, but she can insert a chicken pun into any conversation. Also, thanks to the team at St. Martin's Press—Michael Connor, Geraldine Van Dusen, Alice Baker, and Joan Higgins. Special thanks to James Sinclair for the design and layout of the book and to Steve Snider for the jacket.

Many thanks to Cynthia Nunan and her mother, Mary Ziavras, for the Greek cooking class.

The photos were taken in my home and garden. I can't say enough good things about my photographer and friend, Ben Fink. Thanks to Lucy Lacoste and Simone Williamson for loaning props, and to Alison Saylor and Marilyn Harte for eggs from their hens. Friends Spencer Webb, Ingrid Wheeler, Sharyl Stropkay, and Stephanie Shenton were a huge help.

Lastly, I have to thank my husband, Steve. When we got married, he knew there'd be dogs, but he had no idea that there'd be chickens, too. He enjoys them at least as much as I do. Even though I can't convince him to get ducks, I love him and this life we have.

Book design by James Sinclair
Photographs by Ben Fink

Library of Congress Cataloging-in-Publication Data

Golson, Terry Blonder.
    The farmstead egg cookbook / Terry Golson.
        p. cm.

ISBN-13: 978-0-312-35458-9
ISBN-10: 0-312-35458-4

1. Cookery (Eggs) I. Title.

TX745.G65 2006
641.6'75—dc22   2006040812

First Edition: June 2006

Printed in Mexico

10   9   8   7   6   5   4   3   2   1

Contents

Introduction

I have a small flock of hens in my backyard, but I don't live on a farm. My suburban house is within shouting distance of my neighbors, but I haven't had any complaints. I don't have a rooster that makes a lot of noise. I have peaceful hens that cluck. I keep the henhouse clean and compost the manure. There is no smell and no flies—just cheerful hens and a supply of eggs to use and give away. If you are interested in keeping chickens, all of the information that you need to get started is on my Web site, ww.chickenkeeping.com. (There's even a live Webcam so you can see my hens!)

But perhaps you don't want to keep hens. Perhaps you just want to eat really, really good eggs. Here are some of your options.

Standard Commercial Eggs. Sometimes called "battery layers" or "factory farmed," the hens that lay most of our eggs are housed indoors in small metal cages. The United States Department of Agriculture (USDA) prohibits the feeding of hormones but does allow antibiotics in the daily ration. With refrigerated transport, today's eggs tend to be fresh, although by law they can be packed and shipped thirty days after laying.

Eggs from Free-Range or Cage-Free Hens. The terms *free-range* and *cage-free* are not regulated by the federal government when they are applied to egg-laying poultry. Usually all they mean is that hens aren't kept in wire cages. Many cage-free hens are crowded wing to wing in large barns and never see sunlight or touch real dirt.

As long as the hens have plenty of room, places to take dust baths, clean water, and high-quality feed, staying indoors is not necessarily a terrible thing. But birds are also kept inside for efficiency and to reduce costs, criteria that don't always produce the healthiest hens or the best-tasting eggs.

"Nutritional" Eggs. Some producers claim that their eggs are higher in nutrients such as omega-3 fatty acids, or lower in cholesterol, or have lots of vitamin E. By adjusting the feed, the farmer can get a "nutritional" egg. For example, to get the omega-3 count up, flaxseed is added to the hens' diet. This does not necessarily affect flavor.

Brown, White, and Blue-Green Eggs. The color of the eggshell is related to the color of a chicken's earlobes and has nothing to do with quality or flavor. Araucana hens lay beautiful pastel green and blue eggs that taste the same as common-looking brown eggs.

Organic Eggs. Both federal and state governments regulate the term *organic*. Organic eggs come from hens fed vegetarian, organic feed. Feed affects the color, flavor, and nutrient content of eggs. It also affects cost. Farmers pay a premium for high-quality feed. Since the flavor of the grain goes right through to the eggs, it is well worth the expense.

Farmstead Eggs. Although the term *farmstead* isn't regulated, it is generally understood to define a small family or hobby farm. Farmstead hens are outside during the day. Sometimes hens are kept in a fenced yard—mine are because I have had losses to hawks and raccoons. Other people allow their hens to roam their property. Hens in commercial henhouses are skittish and get stressed when someone unknown comes into their barn. Farmstead hens are happy to see people. My hens are brazenly forward. When someone comes within sight, they dash up to the fence and cluck loudly, as if to say, "What good thing do you have for me?"

Hens stay busy all day. They scratch at the ground, take dust baths, and chase insects. They are very curious and are constantly investigating their environment.

At the end of the day they waddle into the henhouse, settle in next to a best friend, fluff their feathers, and go to sleep.

Farmstead eggs are not necessarily organic. My hens aren't; they get leftover crackers and cereal and cantaloupe seeds. And who knows if that grasshopper that I toss to Edwina has been on the neighbor's fertilized lawn? But if your eggs come from content and busy hens on a small farm, you'll have the best-tasting eggs to be had.

The Quality Difference

I've done blind taste tests of every brand of egg at the supermarket and specialty store. I've hard-cooked eggs from organic growers and from small, local flocks. Every test clearly shows a marked difference between commercial and farmstead eggs. Standard eggs taste faintly metallic, and the yolks have a pallid color and a correspondingly bland flavor. Cage-free eggs vary and sometimes have dark yolks, but usually their flavor is little better than that of standard eggs. On the other hand, yolks from farmstead eggs are usually a brilliant sunflower yellow and have an intense yolky flavor.

Whites from farmstead eggs also have outstanding qualities. They taste clean, with none of the off-flavors found in standard eggs. The USDA grades eggs according to freshness and certain visual criteria. Although the standard for Grade A eggs specifies a "clear" and "viscous" white, in my comparisons that supermarket egg doesn't look anything like my farmstead egg. A farmstead egg white is thick and shimmering white, tinted with yellow. Supermarket egg whites are thin and almost clear when raw. If I crack Twinkydink's egg into a frying pan, it will spread out into a 4-inch oblong. An egg of the same size from the market will spread out $5\frac{1}{2}$ inches or more. This makes a difference with a simple fried egg, but it also matters in any recipe where the whites provide structure and lightness, such as in an angel food cake, a soufflé, or a meringue.

Many organic eggs have these same qualities. Try these good eggs simply prepared—fried or scrambled, poached or hard-cooked—and you will immediately know the difference. It isn't subtle.

A Few Other Things to Know About Farmstead Eggs

Eggs laid in nesting boxes are usually quite clean, but some hens lay eggs on the floor. Eggshells are porous, and if you blast water at the shell, the dirt will go into the egg. A slightly dirty egg should be brushed clean. Dirt that sticks to the shell can be wiped off with a damp cloth.

The porous shell lets in air, and as the egg ages, it releases carbon dioxide and moisture. Over time, the egg will lose flavor and texture and will absorb odors. Eggs bought in closed cartons should stay there; don't transfer them to the refrigerator's open egg bin.

Very fresh eggs will have noticeable chalazae—those opaque sinuous strands in the egg whites that hold the yolks centered. As eggs get older, their chalazae break down. Some people think that chalazae are unsightly. I worked for a chef who had us strain out the chalazae before making omelets. It seemed to me that we lost a lot of egg that way for little benefit. On the other hand, I do strain eggs to make custards silky smooth.

Graded eggs are checked for blood spots, which are tiny dots of discoloration that sometimes form as the egg is laid. Blood spots don't affect flavor but are unsightly. If found, don't discard the egg, just pick out the spot.

Sizes of Eggs

The USDA regulates the sizes of commercial eggs.

Small—$1\frac{1}{2}$ ounces, Medium—$1\frac{3}{4}$ ounces, Large—2 ounces, X-large— $2\frac{1}{4}$ ounces, Jumbo—$2\frac{1}{2}$ ounces

But farmstead eggs come in many sizes, often in the same carton! Our petite Silkie lays eggs that are barely over an ounce. And Ginger, my big black hen with the reddish head, lays eggs that top the chart at almost 3 ounces.

All of my recipes are based on a standard large 2-ounce egg. So if I have

eggs of various sizes, I weigh them until they add up to what would be the standard weight. For example, if I need four eggs, that would be 8 ounces. I might use six of our smallest eggs or just two from Ginger and one from Eleanor.

There is another issue when comparing standard commercial eggs to farmstead eggs. A standard large egg contains a yolk that weighs about half an ounce (33 percent of the liquid weight of the egg). But this proportion does not stay constant as the size of the egg changes. Jumbo eggs have a smaller proportion of yolk to white than do smaller eggs. The opposite is true for small eggs, which are up to 44 percent yolk. Tweedledum's yolk is almost the same size as one from Edwina, our large Barred Plymouth Rock!

A higher proportion of yolks does make a pronounced difference in a recipe. For example, an omelet made from all small eggs will taste intensely of yolks. A pound cake made with small eggs will be denser and softer than a cake made from extra-large eggs.

As a general rule, one standard large egg is about 1/4 cup of volume. One yolk is just over a tablespoon, and one white is just under three tablespoons.

A Note on Egg Safety

There is a very slight chance of catching salmonella or other bacterial disease from undercooked eggs. If you are pregnant or have a compromised immune system, you might want to avoid the recipes with raw eggs.

I eat soft-cooked eggs and raw meringues, and I treat myself to the uncooked cookie batter out of bowls. What I don't do is leave eggs out unrefrigerated, and I am careful to keep recipes with raw eggs, such as homemade mayonnaise, chilled.

So go out and get the best eggs that you can locate and try some of the recipes in this book. And if you can, spend time with some hens.

Anytime Egg Snacks

Midmorning, when I'm ready for something to eat to keep me going, I'll grab a hard-cooked egg and dip it in some seasoned salt. Or if I'm lucky, there will be a couple of deviled eggs in the fridge to snack on. Late afternoon I'll have a cup of tea and a slice of toasted challah. It's always a good time for eggs.

Hard-Cooked Eggs

Is a recipe for boiled eggs necessary? Yes! If you've ever had a tough egg that you were tempted to bounce instead of eat, or an egg with a green yolk, or an egg that you couldn't peel, these directions are for you.

That unsavory-looking green tinge to a hard-cooked egg yolk is due to a reaction of the iron and sulfur in the egg yolks that occurs at high heat. Prevent that by using this method, which cooks but doesn't boil the eggs. That same lower temperature will yield a firm but not rubbery texture.

Fresh hard-cooked eggs are notoriously hard to peel. Try removing the shell from an egg laid the previous day, and you'll end up tossing out half of the white along with the shell. As an egg ages, the membrane around the white begins to separate from the shell. This allows for easier peeling. However, as an egg ages the flavor deteriorates, so the best eggs to hard-cook are between one to two weeks old.

To hard-cook eggs:

1. Place the eggs in a pot and cover with 2 inches of water. Bring the water to a simmer. Don't let the water come to a rolling boil. As soon as the water is simmering, cover the pot and remove from the heat. Set a timer for 12 minutes for small, 16 minutes for large, and 18 minutes for jumbo eggs.
2. Meanwhile, fill a bowl with ice water.
3. When the timer goes off, drain the water out of the pot. Then shake the pot back and forth so that the eggshells crackle all over. Immediately immerse the eggs in the ice water. The water will seep under the shells and loosen them from the whites.
4. When the eggs are cold to the touch, remove them from the water and peel. Any tiny pieces of shell stuck to the eggs can be rinsed off under the tap. Store in a covered container in the refrigerator for up to 4 days for optimum quality.

Tea Eggs

Here, hard-cooked eggs are steeped in tea that is infused with Asian flavors. After a long marinade, the shelled eggs look like marble. If I have a party coming up, I save the eggs from our bantam hens. These small eggs are the right size to serve as finger food. Put them on a platter with a bowl of Szechwan Pepper Salt (page 12) to dip them in. Tea eggs are also very good on a bed of sesame noodles.

Orange pekoe tea gives an authentic Chinese flavor, but you can experiment with other teas. I've used a strong black tea, and the resulting eggs tasted wonderful.

6 eggs
4 cups boiling water
4 bags orange pekoe tea
1 tablespoon soy sauce
1 tablespoon kosher salt
2 star anise
1 large slice fresh gingerroot (unpeeled if desired)

1. Hard-cook the eggs according to the directions on page 9, but do not crack the eggshells before immersing the cooked eggs in ice water.
2. Meanwhile, boil the water and place the tea bags, soy sauce, salt, star anise, and gingerroot in a heatproof bowl. Pour in the boiling water and stir.
3. Remove the eggs from the ice water. Gently crack the shells all over but do not peel. Put the eggs into the tea bath. Cover and refrigerate for at least 24 or up to 48 hours. Discard the liquids and shell the eggs.

Yield: 6 eggs

Seasoned Salts

Hard-cooked eggs and salt are made for each other. When served with a selection of seasoned salts, hard-cooked eggs become special enough for a party. I also like to have seasoned salts on hand for everyday cooking. Put a touch in scrambled eggs, dust on fish, or try the Szechwan pepper salt with some stir-fried vegetables. Seasoned salts are the essence of farmstead cooking—a few simple ingredients of excellent quality prepared with care but not fuss. Stored in airtight jars out of direct sunlight, these salts stay fresh for several months.

• Three-Pepper Salt •

$\frac{1}{2}$ cup kosher salt
1 teaspoon white peppercorns
2 tablespoons pink peppercorns
1 tablespoon green peppercorns

1. Put all the ingredients in a medium sauté pan and place over medium heat. Toss and toast until the salt begins to color. Remove from the pan and let cool.
2. Grind in a spice mill or processor.
3. Store in a glass jar.

• Citrus Salt •

If you don't dry your own citrus peels, dried orange and lemon peel can be found in jars in the spice section of the supermarket.

½ cup kosher salt
1 tablespoon dried lemon peel
2 teaspoons dried orange peel
1 teaspoon dried thyme
1 teaspoon celery seed
1 teaspoon paprika

Grind all the ingredients in a processor until fine. Store in a glass jar.

• Szechwan Pepper Salt •

½ cup kosher salt
¼ cup Szechwan peppercorns
2 teaspoons coriander seeds
1 tablespoon Chinese 5-spice powder

1. Heat a dry, heavy skillet. Add the salt, peppercorns, and coriander seeds. Toast until fragrant but not browned, about 3 minutes. Shake the pan as they toast. Stir in the 5-spice powder. Remove to a bowl and let cool.
2. Grind in a food processor until fine. Sift through a fine-meshed sieve to remove the coarse bits of peppercorn husks.
3. Store in a glass jar.

Pickled Beets and Eggs

Eggs don't get any prettier than this. The whites absorb the beet juice and turn purple, and yet the yolks remain bright yellow. Not only are these beautiful, but they taste great, too. Add pickled eggs to a green salad, use them in the Cobb Salad on page 43, or serve them quartered with the beets as part of an antipasto plate.

6 to 12 hard-cooked eggs, peeled
8 small beets, cooked, peeled, and quartered, or one 15-ounce can whole
    beets, drained
1½ cups apple cider vinegar
1½ cups water
2 teaspoons kosher salt
2 tablespoons sugar
1 teaspoon yellow mustard seeds
½ red onion, sliced

1. Place the eggs and beets in a glass container or jar with a tight-fitting lid.
2. Place the remaining ingredients in a small saucepan and bring to a boil for 3 minutes. Remove from the heat and let cool to lukewarm.
3. Pour the contents of the pot over the eggs and beets. Refrigerate for at least a day. Eat within 2 weeks.

Yield: 6 to 12 servings

Classic Deviled Eggs

Not only have deviled eggs never gone out of style, but they also suit any event, from a picnic to an elegant cocktail party. This is the basic version. Leave as is or dress it up with crème fraîche, goat cheese, caviar, chutney, or smoked salmon. It's hard to go wrong with deviled eggs!

6 hard-cooked eggs, peeled
2 tablespoons mayonnaise
½ teaspoon Dijon mustard
¼ teaspoon dry yellow mustard (such as Coleman's)
¼ teaspoon kosher salt
⅛ teaspoon freshly ground pepper
½ tablespoon sweet pickle relish
Sweet paprika for garnish

1. Slice the eggs in half lengthwise. Remove the yolks and put them in a small bowl.
2. Using a fork, mash the mayonnaise, mustards, salt, and pepper with the egg yolks. Combine until smooth.
3. Stir in the relish until it is evenly distributed.
4. Put the filling in a plastic sandwich bag. Cut off a corner and squeeze the filling into the egg whites. If desired, use a pastry bag with a decorative tip. Dust with paprika.

Yield: 12 eggs

Curried Shrimp Deviled Eggs

Wild-caught shrimp have better flavor and are a more environmentally sound choice than farm-raised shrimp.

6 large hard-cooked eggs, peeled
2 tablespoons mayonnaise
½ teaspoon kosher salt
¼ teaspoon Asian chili paste
1½ teaspoons lime juice
2 teaspoons chopped fresh cilantro
½ teaspoon ground cumin
½ teaspoon curry powder
16 small shrimp, cooked and shelled
Fresh cilantro leaves for garnish (optional)

1. Slice the eggs in half lengthwise. Remove the yolks and put them in a small bowl.
2. Using a fork, mash the egg yolks with the remaining ingredients (except for the shrimp) until smooth.
3. Finely mince 4 of the shrimp and stir into the yolk mixture.
4. Put the filling in a plastic sandwich bag. Cut off a corner and squeeze the mixture into the egg whites. Top each egg with a shrimp. If desired, garnish each with a cilantro leaf.

Yield: 12 eggs

Challah

Many cultures have eggy breads: The Greeks make thalia, a special sweet loaf for Easter; Germans prepare stollen; Italians bake panettone, a rich bread studded with citrus. I grew up with challah, the braided Jewish egg bread, which in many homes is first blessed and then eaten every Friday night. The smell of dough baking in the oven is a welcome transition from work and school to the more relaxed weekend.

A while back I worked in a bakery that made challah. A few customers bought braided loaves for their Sabbath meals. Many more bought the loaves that we fashioned into adorable bears. Challah is a very easy dough to shape, and the egg glaze gives it a mahogany-like finish. Baked loaves freeze well, but, better yet, turn the leftovers into French toast or bread pudding. Even if you don't have a Sabbath tradition, this bread is worth baking.

This recipe uses instant yeast, which does not require "proofing" (being dissolved in warm water). Also note that this recipe uses bread flour, which is sometimes labeled "bread machine flour." Its higher gluten content gives the bread more lift and structure.

> 4 teaspoons (2 packages) instant yeast
> 7 to 8 cups bread flour
> 2 teaspoons kosher salt
> $\frac{1}{2}$ cup sugar
> $1\frac{3}{4}$ cups plus 1 teaspoon water
> 3 large eggs
> $\frac{1}{3}$ cup vegetable oil
> 1 egg yolk

1. Stir the yeast, 1 cup of flour, salt, and sugar together in a large bowl.
2. Pour in the $1\frac{3}{4}$ cups of water and combine. Add the eggs and oil. Mix until smooth.

3. Add the remaining flour, 1 cup at a time, until a sticky dough forms. Knead, adding a little flour at a time, to form a smooth ball of dough. Err on the side of a moist dough. I use a stand mixer for the kneading, but it is an easy dough to work by hand.

4. Put the dough in a covered bowl (I use a large plastic tub with a lid) and let it rest in a warm place until double in bulk. This will take anywhere from 1 to 2 hours depending on the room's temperature. Don't rush it.

5. Punch down the risen dough and, if sticky, dust with flour so that it can be handled. Put on a floured surface and knead briefly until smooth. Divide into 2 portions and then divide those into 3 parts. As they do in professional bakeries, I use a scale to do this, because strands of equal size produce a braided loaf that rises evenly and looks beautiful.

6. Roll each portion into a strand about 12 inches long. Line a large baking sheet with parchment paper.

7. Take 3 of the strands and pinch the ends together. Braid them and then pinch the other end. Tuck the pinched ends under the loaf and place on the parchment. Repeat with the second loaf. Both should fit on the baking sheet or use 2 sheets. Give the loaves room to rise and spread.

8. Mix the egg yolk with 1 teaspoon of water to make an egg wash. Paint the loaves using a pastry brush. Let rise until about double in size, about 1 hour.

9. Meanwhile, preheat the oven to 350 degrees. Just prior to baking, brush the loaves again with the egg wash. Bake for 30 to 40 minutes, until golden brown.

Yield: 2 loaves

Egg Salad with Chives

There are times when a classic creamy and mellow egg salad is exactly right. Use it for sandwiches or atop a bed of greens or along with a selection of vegetable salads. Leftovers invariably become an afternoon snack, scooped right out of the bowl with crackers.

Use this recipe as a guide, but feel free to improvise. For a garden club potluck I picked tarragon, chives, basil, and bronze fennel from my garden, finely minced these herbs, and mashed them with the eggs and a touch of mayonnaise. People loved it and asked, "What's in here?" The answer was easy: a few fresh herbs and very good eggs. Pickle relish is also good when mixed into egg salad—especially if the relish was bought at a farmstand.

4 large hard-cooked eggs, peeled and quartered
$1/4$ cup mayonnaise
$1/8$ teaspoon kosher salt
$1/8$ teaspoon freshly ground pepper
1 tablespoon minced fresh chives
1 tablespoon minced fresh parsley
2 tablespoons minced celery (from half a rib)

1. Mash the eggs and mayonnaise together with a fork until it is the desired consistency. I like it uneven and chunky. If you want it tidy and smooth, start with thinly sliced eggs.
2. Add the remaining ingredients and stir with a fork until combined.

Yield: filling for 2 sandwiches

Morning Eggs

There are few better ways to start the day than eggs and toast. Small-town cafés and diners know this, and many such restaurants base their entire business on breakfast and the humble egg. Fancy hotel dining rooms know this, and you won't find a "power breakfast" at such an establishment without that all-important egg. No need, though, to leave home for your eggs. For little more trouble than opening a box of cereal, you can cook up a fried egg. Take a few more minutes and an omelet or scrambled eggs with sausage can be prepared. And don't forget that pancakes and French toast wouldn't be what they are without eggs. All very nice ways to start the day.

Soft-Cooked Eggs

There is something indulgent about eating a soft-cooked egg right out of the shell. It has to do with the silky texture of the white balanced against the barely oozing rich yolk. Serve in a beautiful eggcup with a dusting of Seasoned Salt (see pages 11–12), and your basic egg is transformed. Not bad for a preparation that requires only a pot of simmering water and a few minutes.

1. Bring a pot of water to a boil. Add the egg(s) and immediately cover and remove from the burner.
2. Let the egg sit in the hot water for 3 to 4 minutes. Using tongs or a slotted spoon, remove each egg and place it in an eggcup. If set in the cup with the narrow end down, there will be a large opening for your spoon or to dip your toast.
3. Take a knife or spoon and tap along the top of the egg to break the shell and remove the top of the egg. There are tools made for this purpose that will make a clean slice, but I think that a ragged edge looks attractively rustic. Use a spoon to eat the egg right out of the shell. Small eggs will require tiny spoons. I like to coddle the largest eggs, which means the ones from our big, brown, red-headed hen, Ginger. If I'm lucky, she'll have laid an egg with a double yolk.

Poached Eggs

Poached eggs are soft free-form egg packets. Rarely made at home, they are most often seen on restaurant brunch menus in eggs Benedict. This is too bad because poached eggs are easy to prepare and can be used in any number of ways. These directions are for poaching four eggs at a time. You can poach several batches of eggs in the same liquid until it becomes cloudy from strands of egg white.

2 teaspoons white wine vinegar
1 teaspoon kosher salt
4 eggs

1. Fill a saucepan with water 3 inches deep. Add the vinegar and salt. Bring to a simmer. Lower the temperature so that the water is just moving.
2. Crack an egg into a small bowl. Slip the egg into the hot water. If the egg sticks to the bottom, gently release it with a spatula. Add each egg in this way. Do not crowd. As the eggs cook, the whites will solidify. Don't worry if they look messy with strands. Poach 3 minutes for a soft-cooked egg with a runny yolk or up to 6 minutes for a firm yolk. Once the eggs are set to your liking, use a slotted spoon to remove them. Dip each egg in a bowl of cold water. This will rinse off the vinegar and stop the cooking.
3. If desired, take kitchen scissors and trim the ragged egg whites. Poached eggs can be refrigerated for up to a day. To store, place the eggs in a bowl of cold water and keep refrigerated until you are ready to reheat them. To reheat, slip the eggs into water that is hot but not simmering (150 degrees) until warmed through. They can also be held in this hot water bath for 30 minutes before serving.

Yield: 4 eggs

Scrambled Eggs

For perfect scrambled eggs you don't need anything other than really good fresh eggs—although it doesn't hurt to use that entire tablespoon of butter, too. Sure, you can cook up scrambled eggs in a nonstick pan spritzed with nonstick cooking spray, but give yourself a treat and use the butter. How incredibly delicious just two ingredients—eggs and butter—can be! Finish off with salt and pepper. Three-Pepper Salt (page 11) is very good dusted on scrambled eggs.

This recipe can be doubled and still be cooked in a 10-inch skillet. However, don't cook more than eight eggs at a time in a 10-inch skillet or some of the eggs will overcook as the rest are setting. A larger pan can of course handle more eggs, but make sure it is a heavy skillet that radiates heat evenly.

1 tablespoon unsalted butter
4 large eggs
Salt to taste

1. Heat a 10-inch skillet over low heat and melt the butter until it just begins to bubble but doesn't brown.

2. Whisk the eggs, then pour them into the pan. Stir frequently, pushing the eggs from the center to the sides of the pan so that raw egg moves into contact with the hot skillet. The trick to scrambled eggs is to cook them over low heat. This allows the eggs to set without squeezing out liquid and drying out the eggs. Serve as soon as the eggs firm up. Add salt to taste. Do not keep warm on a steam table. Eggs at restaurant buffets are often prepared from "whole liquid eggs with color stabilizer," which is why they can be left in a chafing dish for hours. Your eggs at home won't last like that, thank goodness. Serve these eggs as soon as they've been cooked.

Yield: 2 servings

Matzo Brei

During Passover, an eight-day Jewish holiday, Jews can't eat leavened bread, but they can have matzo. For breakfast, instead of scrambled eggs and toast, they often have matzo brei. Looking at this recipe, you might wonder, why bother? The ingredients—bland crackers, eggs, salt, and butter—don't look that interesting. But all together they are! The texture of crackers and eggs fried up in a skillet is perfect. And once cooked, the saltiness is balanced with jam or sugar—or both.

This recipe makes one serving, but you can expand it and cook up to four servings at a time.

1 matzo
1 large egg
¼ teaspoon kosher salt
1 tablespoon unsalted butter or oil
Jam or sugar

1. Break the matzo into large pieces over a colander in the sink. Pour cold water over the pieces for about 30 seconds. Let drain and then squeeze the excess water out of the crackers. This will crumble the matzo but shouldn't turn it to mush.
2. In a small bowl, beat the egg with a fork. Stir in the salt. Stir in the moistened matzo.
3. Heat the butter in a nonstick skillet or well-seasoned cast-iron pan over medium heat, a little hotter than you would cook scrambled eggs because you want the edges of the matzo to crisp. Wait until the butter melts and begins to foam, then add the egg and matzo mixture. Cook, stirring occasionally to break up the eggs. Serve immediately. On the breakfast table have a saltshaker, sugar bowl, and jar of jam. Be generous with all the toppings.

Yield: 1 serving

Scrambled Eggs with Sausage, Cheddar, and Peppers

Imagine a leisurely Sunday morning reading the paper. No pressure to do anything or go anywhere. Now imagine that scene with a plate of these scrambled eggs in front of you, plus toast, orange juice, and a mug of strong coffee on the side. Some of the best things in life can be had right at home.

8 ounces sweet or hot Italian sausage
1 cup chopped bell peppers; use a combination of green, red, and yellow
1 tablespoon unsalted butter
6 large eggs
2 tablespoons milk
½ cup grated sharp cheddar cheese

1. Remove the sausage from the casing and break it into pieces. Cook in a non-stick skillet or well-seasoned cast-iron pan until browned. Remove to a plate.
2. Add the peppers to the pan and cook over medium heat until softened. Set the peppers aside with the sausage. If using pork sausages, there will be a lot of grease in the skillet. Pour it out so that only a thin coating remains. If using low-fat chicken sausage, you might have to add some of the butter in order to sauté the peppers.
3. Whisk the eggs and milk together. Melt the remaining butter in the pan. Pour in the eggs. Stir occasionally until the eggs are half-set. Add the sausage and peppers. Cook until softly set.
4. Stir in the cheese. Cook briefly until the cheese begins to melt.

Yield: 4 servings

Fried Eggs

There are three styles of fried eggs: sunny-side up, over easy, and over hard. How you like your eggs is a personal choice. Whichever way you prefer them, you'll notice a difference when you fry one from a farmstead. Crack a commercial egg, and it spreads out thinly, often over 6 inches across. Crack a farmstead egg, and the whites are thick and the yolk stands up tall. This makes quite a difference in cooking because a thin egg will overcook and toughen in the skillet. On the other hand, a farmstead egg will take longer to set and will end up firm yet not rubbery.

A secret to perfectly cooked eggs is to keep the heat low. Low temperatures allow the egg to solidify without losing moisture. This rule is especially true for fried eggs. Even the butter for fried eggs should be melted in the skillet over low heat so that it bubbles but doesn't brown.

The fat used to grease the pan makes a difference. You can fry an egg in a nonstick skillet and slip it off with a spatula, but without grease, that egg will look like a plastic toy from a play set. Butter adds flavor and moisture. You don't need much. Oil can be used and is good for those who like crispy edges since oil will promote browning. And a camping trip wouldn't be the same without eggs cooked in bacon grease over a hot camp stove.

• Sunny-Side Up •

These eggs are picture-perfect. The whites are bright, with none of the browning that comes from flipping the egg over, and the spherical yolks look like little suns (hence the name). Melt enough butter to coat the pan generously (a heavy nonstick pan is best). Have the heat on low. Crack the egg into the pan and cover with a lid. Cook for 3 to 4 minutes, until the outer yolk firms up and the center remains soft and a touch runny.

• Over Easy •

Melt the butter in a skillet over medium-low heat. Crack the egg in the pan and cook until the white is done all the way but the yolk is still runny, about 1 minute. Use a spatula to flip the egg over. Cook 1 to 2 minutes more, until the edges of the yolk begin to solidify but the inside remains soft.

• Over Hard •

These eggs are for those who don't like runny yolks. The trick here is to set the yolk without having the white turn tough and rubbery. Cook the same as over easy, making sure the temperature is quite low. Once you've flipped the egg, keep cooking until the yolk is thoroughly set, about 3 minutes.

Birdie in a Basket

One of my earliest memories is of eating Birdie in a Basket. Others call it "One-Eyed Egyptian" or "Toad in a Hole." Frying an egg in a hole torn out of a piece of bread is a whimsical, appealing way to serve eggs. As a child, I never would have eaten a lone fried egg, but I happily ate a birdie in a basket whenever it was put in front of me.

Use any type of bread, sliced at the thickness you like.

Unsalted butter
1 slice bread
1 egg

1. Generously butter the bread on both sides. Tear or cut a hole from the center of the bread or use a cookie cutter, such as a heart shape, to cut out the "basket."

2. Heat a skillet and add just enough butter to coat the surface. Put in the slice of bread and then crack the egg into the hole. Cook over medium heat until the bottom sets and the bread toasts. Turn over and continue to cook to the desired doneness.

3. Slip the bread and egg onto a plate. If you used a cookie cutter, fry the cutout center piece, too, and set it next to the egg on the plate. Serve with salt and pepper.

Yield: 1 serving

Fried Egg Sandwich

This recipe is just what a fried egg sandwich should be. In quality, flavor, and texture it is nothing like the fast-food version. Make this as is or use as a base for other additions. Try leftover aioli spread (page 81) on the English muffin or use sliced tomato and mozzarella cheese instead of the bacon and cheddar.

1 to 2 teaspoons unsalted butter
1 egg
1 English muffin
Kosher salt
Freshly ground black pepper
1 slice Canadian bacon
1 slice cheddar cheese

1. Melt the butter in a nonstick or well-seasoned cast-iron skillet set over medium-low heat. Use enough butter to coat the surface of the pan. Crack the egg into the skillet and cook until the egg white sets and the yolk begins to firm, about 2 minutes.
2. Flip the egg over and cook until the yolk is thoroughly set, about 3 minutes more. At the same time, toast the English muffin. When the muffin is toasted, set the egg on the bottom half. Salt and pepper to taste.
3. Increase the heat and fry the bacon until one side browns. Turn it over and top with the cheese. When the bacon is cooked and the cheese has melted, use a spatula to slip it on top of the egg. Top with the other English muffin half.

Yield: 1 serving

Huevos Rancheros

I don't claim that these are totally authentic huevos rancheros, but they are delicious and very easy to make. The addition of cheese makes them more of a complete meal. Queso Fresco is a delicious salty, tart, and dry Mexican cheese. It's worth a trip to a cheese store to find it. Feta is similar and would also be good here.

2 tablespoons salsa
About 2 teaspoons vegetable oil
1 egg
One 5-inch corn tortilla
1 tablespoon grated Queso Fresco

1. Heat the salsa in the microwave until hot but not bubbling. Keep warm.
2. Pour enough oil into a small cast-iron or nonstick skillet to lightly coat the surface. Over medium heat, fry the egg until it is as firm as desired. Remove to a plate.
3. Heating a tortilla in oil can be tricky. The goal is to have a warm, pliable base to put the egg on. Too little oil, and the tortilla will be tough; too much, and it will be greasy. It also must be eaten right away, so cook the tortilla after you've fried the egg. To cook, heat about 1 teaspoon of oil in the skillet over medium-high heat. As soon as the tortilla buckles, turn it over and cook the other side. Immediately put the tortilla on a plate. Place the egg in the center, spoon on the salsa, and top with the cheese.

Yield: 1 serving

Smoked Trout Omelet

There are many ways to cook omelets. Short-order cooks spread a thin layer of eggs on the griddle and then fold it over to get a rectangle. When I worked the brunch service at a fancy café, we made overstuffed omelets in a skillet and at the last minute puffed them in the broiler. The French make a small omelet of only two or three eggs, which is cooked in a lot of butter. The eggs are shaken back and forth as they set, and then with a flick of the wrist they are folded over into a soft omelet. This "rolled technique" takes practice. The method below creates the same omelet but requires less skill and less butter.

> 2 large eggs
> 1 tablespoon milk
> 1 teaspoon minced fresh chives
> ¼ cup shredded smoked trout
> 2 teaspoons unsalted butter

1. Whisk the eggs and milk together and set aside.
2. Heat a 10-inch nonstick omelet pan over medium-low heat. Melt the butter and swirl it around the pan.
3. Pour the eggs into the pan. As the eggs set, lift the edges with a plastic spatula, tilt the pan, and let the raw eggs run under the set ones. Continue to do this until most of the eggs are softly cooked and there is only a sheen of uncooked eggs on the surface. Do not let the eggs brown.
4. Distribute the chives and trout along the center of the omelet. Cover and cook about 3 minutes, until the eggs are set.
5. Tilt the pan over the serving plate, and as the first third of the omelet settles on the plate, shake the pan and roll the rest of the omelet out so that it folds over itself.

Yield: 1 serving

Apple and Brie Omelet

This omelet requires a tart, firm apple. Granny Smith apples are suitable, but when fall arrives and the local orchards have bushels of just-picked apples, all of which are crispy, juicy, and full of sharp apple flavor, I use those.

1 tablespoon unsalted butter, divided
½ tablespoon brown sugar
¼ tart, firm apple, peeled, cored, and thinly sliced
1 tablespoon raw pecans, whole or large pieces
3 large eggs
1 tablespoon milk
1 ounce Brie cheese

1. In a 10-inch nonstick skillet, melt 1 teaspoon of the butter. Stir in the brown sugar. Sauté the apple slices until softened, then set aside, leaving as much of the butter and sugar in the pan as possible. Add the pecans to the pan and cook a few minutes, until they begin to toast. Set aside. If making multiples of this omelet, do this step for all the apples and nuts needed in one batch and then cook the individual omelets.

2. Whisk the eggs and milk together. Cut the Brie into cubes. You should have ¼ cup.

3. Melt the remaining butter in the pan. Pour in the eggs. Cook over low heat, lifting the setting edges of the eggs with a flexible spatula and letting the raw eggs slide under. Continue to do this until it is almost entirely set but not browned.

4. Put the Brie and the apple slices on half of the omelet. Cover and cook over low heat about 4 minutes, until the cheese has melted. Fold the omelet over and slip onto a dish. Top with the pecans.

Yield: 1 serving

Weekend French Toast

The last thing I want to do when I have a houseful of guests on a Sunday morning is stand over a griddle while they're all enjoying themselves. This French toast is the solution. Soak the bread in the batter overnight and then bake it in the oven when everyone wakes up. Not only is it a cinch to make, but the cleanup is easy, too! Serve with warm maple syrup. Or, for a special sauce, gently simmer blueberries and maple syrup, and then push through a sieve to remove the blueberry skins.

    1 loaf (1 pound) **sturdy white bread or challah, unsliced**
    6 large **eggs**
    1 cup **1% milk**
    $1/4$ teaspoon **kosher salt**
    $1/2$ teaspoon **vanilla extract**
    $1/4$ teaspoon **freshly ground nutmeg**
    2 tablespoons **maple syrup (preferably grade B)**

1. Cut the loaf into about ten $3/4$-inch-thick slices.

2. Using a whisk, combine all the ingredients except the bread.

3. Dip each slice of bread in the batter. Place in a flat-bottomed storage dish, stacked up to 3 slices high. Pour the remaining batter over the slices. Cover and refrigerate overnight.

4. Preheat the oven to 400 degrees. Coat 2 baking sheets with nonstick cooking spray. Using a flat spatula, carefully lift the bread out of the storage dish and place the slices on baking sheets in a single layer. Leave space between the slices.

5. Bake for 6 minutes. Turn over. Bake 6 to 8 minutes more, until the egg batter is thoroughly set.

Yield: 5 servings

Cinnamon Sugar Puffed Pancake

Also known as a Dutch Baby Pancake or a German Pancake, this is rich and sweet. The batter rises in the oven like a popover. It looks especially impressive when made in a well-seasoned cast-iron skillet, which can go from the oven to the table. It will begin to deflate as soon as it comes out of the oven, but that is part of its drama and charm.

2 large eggs
¼ cup sugar
⅓ cup whole milk
½ cup all-purpose flour
1 tablespoon unsalted butter
¼ teaspoon ground cinnamon
½ tablespoon confectioners' sugar

1. Preheat the oven to 400 degrees.
2. Whisk the eggs and sugar together. Pour in the milk and continue to whisk. Sift the flour over the mixture and whisk again until smooth. Let the batter sit for 5 minutes.
3. Heat the butter in a 10-inch ovenproof skillet over medium heat. Pour in the batter and cook for 3 minutes.
4. Transfer the skillet to the center of the oven. Bake for 14 minutes, until the edges begin to brown and the center puffs up.
5. Using good oven mitts (the pan will be dangerously hot!), remove the skillet from the oven. Immediately sift the cinnamon and sugar over the pancake.

Yield: 2 large servings

Brunch and Noontime Eggs

Brunch is that in-between time of day when you could have breakfast, but you could also have lunch. It's a time for frittatas stuffed with vegetables, and salads with eggs and potatoes. It's a good time to have sandwiches spread with homemade mayonnaise and layered with egg slices. Sleep a little later and call it all "lunch." In the summer I often have friends gather on our porch for brunch. It seems as if we sit there and eat for hours, from midmorning through lunchtime. We watch the children catch frogs in the small pond and watch the chickens strut in the sun. Before everyone leaves, the kids go into the henhouse to find eggs. They all go home clutching gifts from the hens. (The littlest children have their eggs put into cartons for safekeeping!)

Cobb Salad

You can't go wrong with this classic if you use the best ingredients. If perfectly ripe tomatoes can't be found, then leave them out. Use whatever greens look fresh and crisp. Romaine mixed with mesclun or Bibb and green leaf are well suited to this salad. Get the best slab bacon available. Even selecting a quality red wine vinegar will make a difference.

For the dressing:
2 tablespoons red wine vinegar
4 tablespoons extra-virgin olive oil
¼ teaspoon kosher salt
¼ teaspoon freshly ground pepper
½ teaspoon sugar
1 teaspoon Dijon mustard

For the salad:
4 cups mixed salad greens (about 8 ounces total)
¼ cup chopped fresh herbs (basil, parsley, mint, and chives are good
    options)
4 slices bacon, cooked until crisp and drained
1 ripe avocado, peeled and sliced
4 hard-cooked eggs, peeled and quartered
¼ cup crumbled blue cheese
2 cups sliced deli turkey cut into long strips
2 tomatoes, sliced

1. In a small bowl, whisk together the dressing ingredients.
2. In a large bowl, toss the greens with the fresh herbs. Toss with 2 tablespoons of the dressing. Place the salad on a platter or in a large, shallow serving bowl.
3. Arrange the rest of the ingredients on top of the greens. Use your creativity. A starburst pattern is attractive in a bowl. Or use a rectangular serving platter and arrange the ingredients in alternating strips, making sure that the colors and textures are balanced.
4. Sprinkle the remaining dressing over the top.

Yield: 4 servings

Egg, Potato, and Tuna Salad

This sturdy salad is good as a main course at home or take it to work for a brown bag lunch. Water-packed solid albacore tuna is acceptable here, although oil-packed tuna has more flavor. It's your choice.

8 ounces small new potatoes (red or white)
4 hard-cooked eggs, quartered
One 6-ounce can of tuna, drained
1 rib celery, chopped
¼ cup chopped red onion or scallion
1 tablespoon chopped fresh parsley
1 tablespoon minced fresh dill
1 teaspoon grated lemon zest
½ teaspoon kosher salt
¼ teaspoon freshly ground pepper

For the dressing:
1 tablespoon mayonnaise
1 tablespoon lemon juice
1 tablespoon extra-virgin olive oil
1 tablespoon coarse mustard
1 teaspoon sugar

1. Boil the potatoes until just tender. Let cool and cut into quarters.
2. Put the potatoes and eggs in a bowl. Flake the tuna and add to the bowl. Gently mix these ingredients. Add the celery, onion, parsley, dill, and lemon zest and toss gently. Add the salt and pepper, and stir once more.
3. Whisk the dressing ingredients together until well blended. Pour over the salad and toss to coat.

Yield: 4 servings

Salmon and Egg Pan Bagnat

A pan bagnat is a sandwich that is better the second day, after the oils and flavors have seeped into the bread. Tuna is the usual filling, but I like salmon. The other ingredients can be tweaked as well. In the winter when ripe tomatoes and fresh basil are hard to find, use pesto and roasted red peppers. But always use good eggs! The rich yolks are a soothing counterpoint to the briny olives and the assertive flavor of the salmon.

Any bread that is crusty and rustic will make a good pan bagnat. Regular sandwich bread won't do because the pan bagnat will become soggy and fall apart. Sometimes it is made with a baguette, but I prefer a wider loaf such as an Italian ciabatti.

For the dressing:
3 tablespoons extra-virgin olive oil
1 tablespoon mayonnaise
1 tablespoon lemon juice
2 teaspoons red wine vinegar
1/4 teaspoon kosher salt
1/8 teaspoon freshly ground pepper

For the sandwich:
One 1-pound loaf of crusty bread
One 5-ounce can salmon, drained
1 tablespoon drained capers
1/4 cup pitted and sliced kalamata or niçoise olives
1 tablespoon minced fresh chives, red onion, or scallion
2 tablespoons minced fresh parsley
4 hard-cooked eggs, sliced
2 radishes, thinly sliced
6 large basil leaves, left whole
1/2 ripe tomato, sliced

1. Whisk the dressing ingredients together.
2. Cut the loaf in half lengthwise and brush some of the dressing on each cut side of the bread.
3. With a fork, combine the remaining dressing with the salmon, capers, and olives. Spread the mixture on the bread.
4. Distribute the minced herbs on the mixture. Top with the eggs, radishes, basil, tomato, and the other half of the bread.
5. Slice the loaf into 4 portions. Wrap each tightly with plastic wrap and then with aluminum foil. Refrigerate and eat within 24 hours.

Yield: 4 servings

Bombay Scrambled Eggs

Scrambled eggs don't have to be plain or eaten only at breakfast. In India, scrambled eggs are studded with onions, herbs, and spices. I've specified jalapeño peppers here because they are moderately spicy and are easy to find in the market. But you can use any of a number of fresh hot chili peppers. Try this as a sandwich filling in a pita pocket.

2 tablespoons vegetable oil
1 cup chopped onion
1 clove garlic, minced
6 large eggs
$\frac{1}{2}$ teaspoon kosher salt
$\frac{1}{4}$ teaspoon freshly ground pepper
$\frac{1}{2}$ teaspoon ground cumin
1 fresh jalapeño pepper, seeded and minced (wear rubber gloves)
2 tablespoons chopped fresh cilantro, divided

1. Heat the oil in a large nonstick skillet or well-seasoned cast-iron pan. Sauté the onion and garlic over low heat until very soft and golden.
2. In a bowl, whisk the eggs, salt, pepper, cumin, and jalapeño together. Pour this into the skillet. Stir and cook until the eggs are firm but not dry. Stir in 1 tablespoon of cilantro and serve garnished with the remainder.

Yield: 4 servings

Potato Frittata with Fresh Herbs

Like an omelet, a frittata is a mixture of eggs and filling that cooks in a skillet. But a frittata is not folded over; rather, it sets slowly in the pan. It can handle many more eggs and heavier fillings than a classic French-rolled omelet. Also, frittatas are so dense that they can be sliced into wedges and served at room temperature. I like to offer a selection of different frittatas at brunch. I make them before the guests arrive and display them on cake stands on my kitchen island. I'll also have a basket of breads and muffins, butter, cream cheese, jam, fruit compote, a green salad, and a sweet cobbler or a selection of home-baked cookies.

> 8 ounces red potatoes
> 1 cup sliced red onion
> 1 teaspoon kosher salt
> $1/4$ teaspoon freshly ground pepper
> 5 tablespoons olive oil, divided
> 8 large eggs
> 1 tablespoon minced fresh parsley
> $1/2$ teaspoon minced fresh rosemary
> $1/2$ teaspoon minced fresh thyme

1. Preheat the oven to 425 degrees. Scrub the potatoes and slice them $1/8$-inch thick. Toss the potatoes, onion, salt, and pepper in a bowl with 2 tablespoons of the olive oil. Spread out in a single layer on a baking sheet and cook for 10 to 15 minutes, until browned. Stir once during baking. Remove from the oven and let cool. Lower the oven temperature to 400 degrees.

2. Whisk the eggs and fresh herbs (you can use the same bowl you tossed the spuds in). Stir in the roasted potato mixture. Heat the remaining 3 tablespoons of olive oil in an ovenproof skillet. (You can reduce that to 2 tablespoons if using a nonstick skillet.) Pour in the eggs. Cook over medium-low

heat, covered, for 10 minutes. Slide a flexible heatproof spatula under the eggs every few minutes to keep the bottom from sticking.

3. When the eggs are almost totally set, uncover and put the skillet in the oven. Bake a couple of minutes, until the top sets and is lightly browned. Run the spatula under the eggs and then slip the frittata onto a serving plate. Serve warm or at room temperature, cut into wedges.

Yield: 6 servings

Shirred Eggs with Spinach and Cream

A shirred egg is simply an egg baked uncovered in a buttered dish, usually with a few other components to give it interest. You have your choice of cheese here. Parmesan is a safe option, but this is a good opportunity to use up that little bit of interesting cheese that is languishing in the refrigerator.

This recipe serves one. If making these for a number of people, simply multiply the recipe as needed. Always bake in individual ramekins, although the ramekins can be placed in a baking dish so that they are easy to handle in and out of the oven. Shirred eggs can be assembled and then refrigerated for up to an hour before baking.

> 1 teaspoon unsalted butter
> 2 tablespoons chopped spinach, fresh or frozen
> 1 tablespoon cream (your choice from light to heavy)
> 1 egg
> Kosher salt
> Freshly ground pepper
> Freshly ground nutmeg
> 1 tablespoon grated cheese of your choice

1. Preheat the oven to 350 degrees.
2. Put the butter in a 6- or 8-ounce ovenproof ramekin. Melt it in the microwave (about 20 seconds) and swirl around to coat the bottom and sides.
3. Briefly cook the spinach until wilted, then squeeze out the excess liquid. (This can be done quickly in the microwave.) Put the spinach in the ramekin. Pour in the cream. Crack the egg into the ramekin. Grate salt and pepper onto the egg. Dust on the nutmeg. Top with the cheese.
4. Place the ramekin in the oven and bake about 15 minutes, until the yolk begins to set. Serve hot.

Yield: 1 serving

Asparagus with Poached Eggs and Smoked Salmon

I have two bantam hens, Tweedledum and Snowball. They are the smallest of chickens and lay small eggs, which I save to use in recipes like this. Two small eggs per person make a charming presentation.

For the dressing:
1 teaspoon sugar
1 tablespoon whole-grain mustard
1 teaspoon minced fresh dill for garnish
2 tablespoons lemon juice
2 tablespoons mayonnaise
$1/4$ teaspoon kosher salt
$1/8$ teaspoon freshly ground pepper
$1/3$ cup vegetable or olive oil

For the assembled dish:
4 toast slices
8 ounces smoked salmon
12 asparagus spears, steamed
4 large poached eggs (directions on page 25)
Fresh chopped dill for garnish

1. Whisk the dressing ingredients together.
2. Assemble this recipe on individual dinner plates. Put a piece of toast on each plate. Arrange the salmon and asparagus on each piece of toast. Top with the egg. Drizzle the dressing over the egg and asparagus. Garnish with dill.

Yield: 4 servings

Poached Eggs in Twice-Baked Potatoes

This is great for a brunch crowd because it can be assembled a day ahead and baked just before the company arrives.

1 large baking potato (between ¾ to 1 pound)
¼ cup shredded cheddar or Monterey Jack cheese
2 tablespoons sour cream
2 teaspoons unsalted butter, softened
1 slice bacon, cooked until crisp and drained
¼ teaspoon kosher salt
⅛ teaspoon freshly ground pepper
2 eggs
1 tablespoon grated Parmesan cheese
1 tablespoon sliced chives or scallions for garnish (optional)

1. Preheat the oven to 375 degrees. Scrub the potato so it is very clean and then bake until a knife can be easily inserted in the center. Allow the potato to cool so it can be handled.
2. Cut the potato in half lengthwise. If necessary, cut off a small slice from the bottom of each half so that the potatoes sit flat. Scoop out the potato to ¼ inch from the skin. (A serrated grapefruit knife makes easy work of this task.) Set aside ¼ cup of the potato for this recipe, reserving any remaining potato for another use.
3. Combine the potato, cheese, sour cream, and butter. Mash until mostly smooth. Crumble in the bacon and stir until it is evenly distributed. Stir in the salt and pepper.
4. Mound the filling in each potato half. Make an indentation in the center for the egg. Place the potatoes in a baking dish.

5. Using the directions on page 25, poach the eggs for 1 minute so that the white is set but the yolk remains runny. Put a poached egg in the hollow of each potato half. Sprinkle the Parmesan on top.

6. Bake in a 375-degree oven for 10 minutes, or until the cheese begins to brown. Garnish with the chives or scallions.

Yield: 2 servings from each potato; multiply as needed

Shirred Eggs on Polenta

Shirred eggs are usually very rich and made with cream. Not this version. Here the egg is baked on a bed of polenta and vegetables.

Jarred bruschetta topping is available in gourmet stores and at farmstands. There are many versions, some with a variety of vegetables, some with just tomatoes. With a jar on hand, this recipe takes less than a minute of preparation, but I've also supplied a recipe. Either way, serve with a thick slice of toast and a salad, and you have a hassle-free meal.

½ teaspoon olive oil
One 1-inch slice polenta (from a log of prepared polenta, found in many supermarkets)
1½ tablespoons bruschetta topping, jarred, or use the recipe on facing page.
1 egg
Kosher salt
Freshly ground pepper
1 tablespoon grated Parmesan cheese

1. Preheat the oven to 350 degrees.
2. Swirl the olive oil in a 6-ounce ramekin to coat the bottom and sides.
3. Place the slice of polenta in the bottom of the ramekin. Spoon on the bruschetta topping. Crack an egg into the ramekin. Grind salt and pepper over the egg. Sprinkle on the Parmesan.
4. Place in the oven for 15 minutes, or until the egg is set.

Yield: 1 serving

Bruschetta Topping

This recipe has many uses. It is wonderful, of course, on shirred eggs or for bruschetta (top hearty bread with it, dust it with cheese, and broil). Try leftovers as the base layer for a casserole of baked chicken thighs, or garnish a thick fish steak with bruschetta topping before broiling.

1 pound ripe tomatoes
1 clove garlic, peeled
$\frac{1}{2}$ cup fresh basil
$\frac{1}{2}$ tablespoon extra-virgin olive oil
$\frac{1}{2}$ teaspoon kosher salt
$\frac{1}{8}$ teaspoon freshly ground pepper
$\frac{1}{8}$ teaspoon red pepper flakes
$\frac{1}{4}$ teaspoon dried or $\frac{1}{2}$ teaspoon fresh minced oregano

1. Core the tomatoes and slice in half across their equators. Squeeze out and discard the seeds.
2. Finely mince the garlic by hand or in a food processor. Chop the tomatoes and basil either by hand or machine. Stir in the remaining ingredients.

Yield: 1$\frac{1}{2}$ cups topping

Salsa and Guacamole Frittata

Frittatas are finished in a hot oven. A nonstick pan allows a frittata to slip out of the skillet, but many nonstick surfaces are not ovenproof. If using a regular skillet, spritz it with nonstick cooking spray before adding the butter, and the frittata will easily come out of the pan.

1 tablespoon unsalted butter
6 large eggs
½ teaspoon kosher salt
3 tablespoons guacamole, prepared
2 tablespoons salsa, drained if watery
2 tablespoons canned black beans, rinsed and drained
3 tablespoons grated cheddar or jack cheese, or Queso Fresco
Sour cream (optional)

1. Preheat the oven to 425 degrees.
2. Place a 10-inch nonstick skillet or well-seasoned cast-iron pan over medium-low heat. Melt the butter.
3. Lightly mix the eggs and salt. Pour into the heated skillet. Cover and cook for 5 minutes. Lift the egg with a spatula several times as it cooks so that it doesn't stick to the bottom of the pan. Let the raw egg flow under the cooked egg.
4. When the egg is halfway set, arrange teaspoonfuls of the guacamole and salsa on top of the frittata. Distribute the beans across the surface. Top with the cheese.
5. Cover and continue to cook gently about 10 minutes more, until the egg is almost entirely set.
6. Place the frittata, uncovered, in the oven and cook for 2 to 4 minutes, until the egg sets and puffs, and the cheese melts. Using good oven mitts, carefully remove the hot pan from the oven. Using a wide spatula, release the frittata from the pan and slip it onto a serving plate. If desired, serve with additional salsa and sour cream on the side.

Yield: 4 servings

Zucchini and Mint Frittata

A frittata can be finished in the oven, or it can be flipped over in the pan and finished on the stove. This recipe gives directions for the stove version, but you can also finish it in a hot oven as in previous recipes.

3 tablespoons olive oil, divided
½ cup sliced onion
1 red bell pepper, sliced julienne
1 pound zucchini (about 3 small), sliced
8 large eggs
¼ cup (4 tablespoons) grated Parmesan cheese, divided
¼ cup chopped fresh mint
½ teaspoon kosher salt
¼ teaspoon freshly ground pepper

1. Heat 2 tablespoons of the olive oil in a 10-inch heavy skillet. Sauté the onion and bell pepper until soft and golden. Take your time on this step to fully develop the sweet flavors of these vegetables. Stir in the zucchini and continue to cook over low heat until the edges begin to brown. Set aside in a bowl.
2. In another bowl, whisk the eggs, 3 tablespoons of the Parmesan, mint, salt, and pepper.
3. Heat the remaining tablespoon of olive oil in the skillet. Pour in the eggs and then distribute the vegetables on top. Cover and cook over medium-low heat about 15 minutes, until the eggs are set but not yet firm on top. Several times while the eggs are cooking, take a flexible spatula and run it along the edge and under the frittata to make sure the eggs are not sticking to the pan.
4. Take the skillet off the heat. Put a dinner plate over it and flip the frittata onto the plate. Then slip the frittata back into the pan, now with the bottom side up. Top with the remaining tablespoon of Parmesan. Cook a few minutes more, until done.

Yield: 6 servings

Gremolata Ricotta Frittata

The bright flavors of gremolata—an Italian mixture of lemon zest, garlic, and parsley—give this frittata a spark.

3/4 cup ricotta cheese
1/4 cup Parmesan cheese
1 clove garlic, minced
3 tablespoons chopped fresh parsley
2 tablespoons chopped fresh basil
1 teaspoon grated lemon zest
1/2 teaspoon kosher salt
1/4 teaspoon freshly ground pepper
6 large eggs
2 cups cooked spaghetti
1 tablespoon olive oil

1. Preheat the oven to 425 degrees.
2. Using a fork, thoroughly combine the cheeses, garlic, parsley, basil, lemon zest, salt, and pepper in a medium-sized bowl.
3. Stir in the eggs and continue to mix with a fork until well combined.
4. Toss in the pasta and stir until it is evenly coated with the egg mixture.
5. Heat the olive oil in a 10-inch ovenproof sauté pan. Pour in the frittata filling, cover, and cook over low heat for 15 minutes. Several times during the cooking, slip a flexible spatula around the edges and partially under the frittata to keep it from sticking. After 10 to 15 minutes, the bottom will be light brown and all but the top should be set.
6. Put the frittata, uncovered, in the oven and bake until the top sets and begins to brown lightly, about 4 to 6 minutes. Remove from the oven with good mitts (the handle will be very hot!) and slip onto a serving plate.

Yield: 4 servings

Chard and Feta Strata

A strata is similar to a frittata, but it gets added bulk and a softer texture from bread. Like a frittata, it can be served hot or at room temperature, as a main course or as an appetizer.

Select chard with unblemished dark leafy greens. Depending on the variety, the stems and veins in the leaves of the chard will vary in color from white to red to orange. Rainbow-hued chard is beautiful but would color this casserole pink, so buy white chard.

1 cup chopped white chard leaves
1 tablespoon olive oil
2 cloves garlic, minced
½ cup chopped red onion
1 tomato
6 large eggs
¼ cup whole milk
2 slices white sandwich bread
1 teaspoon dried oregano
1 teaspoon dried basil
1 teaspoon kosher salt
¼ teaspoon freshly ground pepper
½ cup crumbled feta cheese
1 tablespoon grated Parmesan cheese

1. Wash the chard leaves very well. Swirl the leaves in several changes of water, lifting them out so that any grit falls to the bottom of the bowl they are being washed in. Cut off and discard the tough main stems. Coarsely chop the leaves.
2. Heat the olive oil in a large, heavy skillet. Cook the garlic and onion over low heat for 5 minutes. Add the chard and cook until wilted.

3. Slice the tomato in half and then squeeze out and discard the seeds. Dice the tomato. Use 1 cup for this recipe. Add the tomato to the pan and continue to cook until all the vegetables are softened but not mushy. Put the cooked vegetables in a colander and let drain.

4. Preheat the oven to 350 degrees. Coat a 9-inch round baking dish with non-stick cooking spray. Since this can be served in its casserole, select an attractive dish.

5. Whisk the eggs and milk until combined. Leaving on the crust, cut the bread into $1/2$-inch cubes. Stir the bread, oregano, basil, salt, and pepper into the eggs. Stir in the vegetables and feta cheese.

6. Spread the mixture in the baking dish. Dust with the Parmesan. Bake for 30 to 40 minutes, until puffed and set in the center.

Yield: 6 servings

Quiche with Bacon and Cheese

Slab bacon is thickly cut bacon that is usually not as sweet as regular breakfast bacon.

One 9-inch All-Purpose Pastry Crust (page 100-101)
4 large eggs
1½ cups light cream or half-and-half
½ teaspoon kosher salt
1 cup grated sharp cheddar cheese
3 slices slab bacon, cooked, drained, and crumbled

1. Put the crust in a 9-inch pie plate, preferably glass or ceramic. Prebake the piecrust until it begins to brown. (Follow the directions on page 101.)
2. Preheat the oven to 325 degrees.
3. Using an electric mixer, beat the eggs and cream for 1 minute, until the mixture increases slightly in volume. Stir in the salt, cheese, and bacon. Pour into the pie plate.
4. Bake for 35 to 40 minutes, until the center is just set and the edges begin to brown.

Yield: 6 servings

Basil and Mozzarella Balls Tian

A tian is similar to a quiche, but it doesn't have a crust and is unmolded onto a plate. In this version the mozzarella balls provide small bursts of flavor. Marinated goat cheese balls would also be very good. This tian is slightly smaller than a standard quiche and so is the perfect size for two when you don't want leftovers.

> 5 large eggs
> $^2/_3$ cup light cream
> $^1/_2$ teaspoon kosher salt
> $^1/_4$ teaspoon freshly ground pepper
> 6 basil leaves, sliced
> 6 oil-packed and herb-marinated mozzarella balls
> $^1/_4$ red bell pepper, fresh or roasted, sliced

1. Preheat the oven to 325 degrees. Coat a 1$^1/_2$-quart (about 7 inches round) ceramic baking dish with nonstick cooking spray.
2. Using an electric mixer, beat the eggs and cream for 1 minute. Stir in the salt, pepper, and basil leaves. Pour into the baking dish.
3. Spoon the mozzarella balls out of the oil, drain briefly in a mesh sieve, and then distribute them evenly across the tian.
4. Arrange the sliced peppers over the egg mixture.
5. Bake for 30 to 35 minutes, until the center is set and the edges begin to brown. Use a flexible spatula to loosen the tian from the dish. Invert onto a plate and then invert once more onto a serving dish.

Yield: 2 servings

Evening Eggs

At my house there's never "nothing in the house for dinner." We can always have eggs. Many recipes, such as Egg Drop Soup (page 88), use pantry staples and take only a few minutes to prepare. Vegetable Fried Rice (page 73) makes use of leftover rice and whatever vegetables are on hand. Swordfish Kabobs with Aioli (page 81) and Spaghetti alla Carbonara (page 77) are hearty entrees. And on a wintry night there is nothing more warming and satisfying than Spanish Garlic Soup (page 90). Although these meals feature eggs, they don't look anything like breakfast!

Fried Eggs and Goat Cheese

This is a favorite summer dinner. When it's time for supper, I head to the garden and henhouse. In the late afternoon most of the hens are busy outside. But Snowball, my son's tiny bantam White Leghorn who almost never lays an egg, will be inside sitting on four big brown eggs that her little body can barely cover. Snowball rasps a warning at me but lets me shift her over and collect the eggs. Then she settles down again as if there are still lumpy eggs under her. I thank her and go to the garden, grab a tomato and some herbs, and go back to the house with my treasures. Dinner will be ready in a few minutes.

2 tablespoons dried bread crumbs
½ teaspoon kosher salt
2 ounces goat cheese, crumbled (⅓ cup)
2 teaspoons olive oil
1 large ripe tomato, diced
¼ cup sliced fresh basil
1 tablespoon chopped fresh parsley
4 eggs

1. Combine the bread crumbs, salt, and goat cheese in a small bowl.
2. Pour enough olive oil in a large nonstick pan to coat the surface. Sauté the tomato, basil, and parsley until the tomato is soft but not mushy. Set aside in a bowl.
3. If necessary, add a touch more olive oil to the pan. Crack the eggs into the pan and top with the cheese mixture. Cook over medium-low heat until the egg whites set. Using a spatula, separate the eggs and flip them over. Top with the sautéed tomatoes. Cook until the yolks are as firm as desired.

Yield: 2 servings

Steak and Eggs with Shallot-Garlic Butter and Sweet Onions

Cooking steak and eggs is fun. I make this in a big cast-iron skillet. The meat sizzles, and the onions and peppers create a mouthwatering aroma. The eggs are fried last in the pan, and they take on the juices from the meat and vegetables. I imagine myself over a cookstove with stars overhead. On summer nights we eat this on the porch and, if lucky, watch the lightning bugs put on a show.

1-pound steak, 1-inch thick
Kosher salt
Freshly ground pepper
1 to 2 tablespoons vegetable oil
1 green bell pepper, sliced
1 clove garlic, sliced
1 sweet onion, such as Vidalia, peeled and sliced
1 tablespoon Shallot-Garlic Butter (page 72)
4 eggs

1. My favorite steak for this is a boneless rib eye, but use whatever looks good at the market. Rub the steak with salt and pepper to taste. A cast-iron skillet is perfect for this sort of recipe, although a large, heavy-bottomed pan will do. Heat the large skillet and pour in enough oil to thoroughly coat the bottom. Cook the steak about 5 to 7 minutes on each side, until done as desired.

2. While the steak is cooking, surround it with the bell pepper, garlic, and onion slices. Cook the vegetables until very soft and golden (about the same time as it takes the steak to cook).

3. Put the vegetables on a serving plate and cover with aluminum foil to keep warm. Put the steak on a cutting board. Top the steak with slices of the shallot-garlic butter and let it rest while cooking the eggs.

4. Fry the eggs in the skillet.

5. Slice the steak and put it on a serving plate with the onions. Set the eggs on the side.

Yield: 4 servings

• Shallot-Garlic Butter •

Try the extra shallot-garlic butter on grilled fish or use it to sauté vegetables.

1 clove garlic
½ teaspoon kosher salt
1 tablespoon minced shallot
1 tablespoon minced fresh parsley
4 tablespoons unsalted butter, softened

1. Using the flat side of a chef's knife, smash the garlic with the salt and then mince until it becomes a paste.

2. Stir the garlic paste, shallot, and parsley into the butter. Put the butter on a piece of plastic wrap, shape it into a narrow log, wrap tightly, and refrigerate until solid. This recipe makes more than is needed for the Steak and Eggs recipe on the previous page. The excess can be kept refrigerated for a week or frozen for two months.

Vegetable Fried Rice

As is, this recipe is just right for a light supper. For a heartier meal add $1/2$ cup of diced cooked chicken or ham or shrimp, or all three.

4 cups cooked white rice	1 cup diced vegetables of choice
3 large eggs	3 tablespoons vegetable oil,
2 teaspoons dry sherry	divided
$1/4$ cup chopped scallions	$1/4$ teaspoon freshly ground
1 rib celery, chopped	pepper
$1/4$ cup diced carrot	$1/2$ teaspoon kosher salt
$1/2$ cup peas, thawed if frozen	1 tablespoon soy sauce

1. The best rice for fried rice is leftover rice from a Chinese restaurant. Or cook the rice the day before so that it has time to dry out. Just before you make this recipe, separate the grains with your fingers and set aside in a bowl.
2. In a small bowl, mix the eggs and sherry until combined.
3. Prepare the scallions, celery, carrots, and peas, and set aside in another bowl.
4. Prepare another cup of vegetables. Most vegetables work well here as long as they are cut into small uniform pieces so that they cook quickly in the pan. Fresh mung sprouts and thinly sliced cabbage are good, too. Put them in the bowl with the other vegetables.
5. Heat a wok or a large skillet over medium heat. Pour in 2 tablespoons of the oil. Add the eggs and stir constantly until scrambled and broken into small lumps.
6. Stir in the rice and cook until the eggs and rice are evenly distributed throughout.
7. Increase the heat, add the remaining tablespoon of oil, and add the remaining ingredients, including the meats if desired. Cook until heated through.

Yield: 2 servings

Fettuccini Alfredo with Rosemary and Garlic

When I worked the lunch line at a little bistro, I loved it when an order for fettuccini Alfredo came through. It was so easy and absolutely foolproof. The head chef was German, and we did an untraditional version with a lot of garlic. No one complained. The rosemary is my addition. I think it needs that pungent bit of herb to balance the rich cream.

1 pound fettuccini
4 tablespoons (½ stick) unsalted butter, divided
2 cloves garlic, minced
1 cup heavy cream, divided
1 cup Parmesan cheese, plus more for garnish
3 egg yolks
½ teaspoon kosher salt
¼ teaspoon freshly ground pepper
1 tablespoon chopped fresh rosemary

1. Bring a large pot of heavily salted water to a boil and cook the fettuccini according to the package directions.
2. Meanwhile, heat 1 tablespoon of butter in a medium sauté pan. Add the garlic and cook over low heat for several minutes. Add the remaining butter and cook until melted.
3. Pour in 3/4 cup of the cream and add the cheese. Stirring frequently, cook for 2 minutes or until thickened.
4. In a small bowl, whisk the egg yolks, the remaining 1/4 cup of cream, salt, and pepper.
5. When the pasta is done, immediately drain it into a large colander. Shake a few times to remove the excess water, then put it in a pasta serving bowl (a

large, shallow bowl). Pour in the cream and cheese mixture and then stir in the egg yolk mixture. Toss quickly so that the pasta is thoroughly coated and the yolks cook.

6. Toss in the rosemary and top with additional Parmesan. Have salt and pepper grinders at the table.

Yield: 4 servings

Spaghetti alla Carbonara

Pancetta is Italian bacon. It isn't smoked or sweetened like American bacon. If you can't find it, use slab bacon.

1 pound spaghetti
3 large eggs
¼ cup grated Romano cheese
½ cup grated Parmesan cheese, plus more for garnish
1 tablespoon olive oil
8 ounces pancetta, cut into ½-inch dice
2 cloves garlic, peeled and smashed
½ teaspoon kosher salt
2 tablespoons sliced fresh basil
¼ teaspoon freshly ground black pepper

1. Bring a large pot of generously salted water to a boil. Cook the pasta according to the package directions.
2. While the pasta is cooking, crack the eggs into a large, shallow serving bowl. Whisk to break up the egg yolks. Stir in the cheeses.
3. Also while the pasta is cooking, heat the olive oil in a skillet. Add the pancetta and garlic. Cook until the pancetta is crispy. Discard the garlic.
4. As soon as the pasta is done, drain it in a colander. Shake a few times to remove the excess water, then put it in the bowl with the eggs and cheese, and toss. The hot pasta will cook the eggs.
5. Add the pancetta with the olive oil to the pasta. Stir in the salt and garnish with the basil. Grate pepper on top. Have extra Parmesan for dusting each portion. Serve immediately.

Yield: 4 large servings

Baked Mayonnaise-Slathered Catfish

This recipe produces very moist baked fish with a crispy exterior.

⅓ to ½ cup homemade mayonnaise (recipe follows)
½ cup dry bread crumbs
1 pound skinless catfish fillets
Olive oil spray

1. Preheat the oven to 375 degrees. Coat a baking sheet with nonstick cooking spray.
2. Put the mayonnaise on a dinner plate and the bread crumbs on another.
3. Wash and dry the fillets. Dip a fillet into the mayonnaise and generously coat both sides. Transfer the fish to the plate with the bread crumbs. Dredge the fish in the bread crumbs and then gently shake off any excess. Put the fillet on the baking sheet. Repeat with the remaining fillets.
4. Lightly coat the fish with olive oil spray. Bake for 12 to 15 minutes, or until done. You can usually tell when a fish fillet is cooked by the color of the flesh and how it flakes apart. Since you don't want to pry apart a breaded fillet, however, to test for doneness touch the center of the fillet with your finger. If it feels as firm as the bottom of the palm of your hand, it is done.

Yield: 3 servings

• Mayonnaise •

If you've never had homemade mayonnaise, how good it is will surprise you. The color will, too: It's yellow, not white like the jarred version. Mayonnaise is made with raw egg yolks, so keep it refrigerated. Use commercial mayonnaise for recipes that will be left out, such as a salad at a picnic. Save the homemade mayonnaise for a special treat at home. It doesn't have to be fancy. There are few lunches better than a homegrown tomato and bacon sandwich made with fresh mayonnaise.

1 large egg
2 egg yolks
1 teaspoon Dijon mustard
1 tablespoon lemon juice
½ teaspoon kosher salt
⅛ teaspoon freshly ground pepper
¾ cup vegetable oil (any high-quality mild-flavored oil)

1. Restaurants make large quantities in the food processor, but it is best to make a small amount by hand. Besides, cleanup is easier—just a whisk and a bowl. Put all ingredients except the oil in a medium bowl and whisk until thick.
2. While whisking constantly, add the oil in a slow, steady stream and continue to whisk until thick. (The mayonnaise will begin to separate after about a day. A brisk whisking can thicken it up again.) Use within 3 days.

Yield: 1 cup

Swordfish Kabobs with Aioli

Aioli is garlicky, lemony homemade mayonnaise. It is rich, smooth, and pungent. It is great as a dip for crudités, a sauce for steamed vegetables, a spread for sandwiches (try it on fried egg and tomato), or, as in this recipe, as the dipping sauce for grilled swordfish skewers.

For the aioli:
4 cloves garlic
$1/2$ teaspoon kosher salt
2 egg yolks
1 teaspoon Dijon mustard
$1/4$ teaspoon freshly ground white or black pepper
3 teaspoons lemon juice
1 cup extra-virgin olive oil

For the kabobs:
2 small summer squash, sliced into 1-inch pieces
1 pint cherry tomatoes
2 green bell peppers, cut into large pieces
1 red onion, peeled and cut into large pieces
1 pound swordfish, cut into large cubes

For the dressing:
$1/4$ cup olive oil
2 tablespoons lemon juice
$1/2$ teaspoon kosher salt
$1/2$ teaspoon freshly ground pepper

1. To make the aioli: Using a chef's knife, mash and mince the garlic with the salt until you get a smooth paste.

2. In a small bowl, whisk the garlic paste and egg yolks. Add the mustard and pepper, and whisk until smooth. Whisk in 1 teaspoon of the lemon juice.

3. Add half of the oil in a slow, steady stream, whisking vigorously until thick. Stir in the remaining 2 teaspoons of lemon juice and then finish whisking in the oil. Because aioli is made with raw egg yolks, it is important to keep it refrigerated and serve it chilled. When it is to be served at a buffet where it would be left out long enough to reach room temperature, eliminate worries by setting the bowl of aioli in a bowl filled with ice.

4. To make the kabobs: Assemble the skewers by adding the items in this order until all have been used: squash, tomato, pepper, onion, swordfish, onion, squash, tomato, and so forth.

5. To make the dressing: Whisk all the ingredients together. Pour over the skewers to coat. These can be refrigerated for up to a day before grilling.

6. Bring the grill to medium heat. Cook the kabobs for about 8 minutes, until the swordfish is just cooked through. Turn the kabobs once or twice during grilling. Serve with aioli on the side.

Yield: 4 servings

Cheese Soufflé

A soufflé is not as temperamental or fussy to make as you might imagine. As long as you have a 1½-quart soufflé dish (a straight-sided round casserole), you can do this.

3 tablespoons unsalted butter, plus more for greasing the dish
1 cup whole milk
3 tablespoons all-purpose flour
⅛ teaspoon ground nutmeg
½ teaspoon kosher salt
⅛ teaspoon freshly ground black pepper
½ teaspoon sweet paprika
6 large eggs, separated, at room temperature
1 cup shredded Swiss cheese

1. Preheat the oven to 375 degrees. Put the rack in the lower third of the oven. Butter a 1½-quart soufflé dish. In the microwave or in a small saucepan, warm the milk until hot but not simmering.

2. In a medium saucepan, melt the butter. Stir in the flour and cook for 2 minutes, until bubbly but not brown. Slowly pour in the hot milk while whisking vigorously. Increase the heat and boil about 3 minutes, until the mixture thickens. Remove from the heat and scrape into a large bowl. Stir in the nutmeg, salt, pepper, and paprika.

3. When the flour mixture is slightly warmer than room temperature, stir in the egg yolks, one at a time. (This base can be made up to a day ahead of time and stored in the refrigerator.)

4. In a clean bowl, using an electric mixer, beat the egg whites and a pinch of salt until stiff peaks form.

5. Scoop out ¼ cup of egg whites and stir it into the base. Then add the rest of the whites to the flavor base. Gently fold these 2 mixtures together, adding

¼ cup of Swiss cheese at a time until fully combined.

6. Spoon the filling into the soufflé pan.

7. Bake for 35 minutes, or until the soufflé rises and forms a sloping, crusty cap and wobbles a bit when pushed. The soufflé will begin to deflate within 3 minutes of being removed from the oven, so bring it right to the table and eat immediately.

Yield: 4 servings

Avgolemono Soup

This Greek soup is lemony, salty, and frothy. It uses the most basic ingredients to create an addictive soup. But avgolemono soup will not work with insipid canned broth. If you don't have good homemade chicken broth, use the best prepared broth you can purchase.

6 cups chicken broth
1 cup orzo or riso pasta
4 large eggs
¼ cup fresh lemon juice
½ to 1 teaspoon kosher salt
Freshly ground pepper to taste
Minced fresh mint and/or sage for garnish

1. Bring the broth to a simmer in a 3- or 4-quart saucepan. Add the orzo, cover, and simmer for 12 minutes. Take off the stove.
2. Using an electric hand mixer, beat the eggs until foamy. Add the lemon juice and continue to beat until frothy.
3. Once the orzo is cooked, scoop out a cup of the hot broth and add it to the egg mixture, beating as you pour it in. Then pour the egg and lemon froth into the soup pot, beating continuously until foamy—the texture of milk in a latte.
4. Taste and add salt and pepper if needed. Eat right away! Ladle into a soup bowl and top with the fresh herbs. As this soup sits, it loses its ethereal quality, but leftovers will still taste good.

Yield: 6 servings

Italian Egg Soup

You won't find this recipe in an Italian cookbook. It's something I came up with that uses Italian ingredients in a way that satisfies me. This soup is thick, deeply flavorful, and easy to prepare, and it uses ingredients that I always have on hand.

3 tablespoons extra-virgin olive oil

½ cup cubed pancetta (from 2 slices)

1 cup chopped onion

2 cloves garlic, minced

6 ounces fresh baby spinach

⅓ cup Arborio rice

6 cups chicken broth

¼ cup grated Romano cheese

4 large eggs

Kosher salt

Freshly ground pepper

Crushed hot pepper flakes

1. Heat the olive oil in a heavy-bottomed 4-quart soup pot. Toss in the pancetta and onion, and cook until the pancetta begins to brown and crisp and the onion softens and turns golden. Add the garlic and cook a few minutes more.

2. Wash the spinach (even if the bag says washed). Discard any mushy leaves. Add the spinach to the pot and cook about 2 minutes, until wilted. Stir in the rice.

3. Pour in the broth and bring to a simmer. Cover and cook at a low simmer for 20 minutes.

4. Using a fork, stir the cheese and eggs together until well combined. Take the pot off the heat and, if desired, pour the soup into a serving tureen. Immediately stir in the egg-cheese mixture. It will cook when it hits the hot soup. Taste and season with salt and pepper if necessary (this will depend on the saltiness of the broth).

5. Dust the soup with a pinch of hot pepper flakes.

Yield: 6 servings

Egg Drop Soup

Restaurant versions of this soup are heavily thickened with cornstarch. This is a lighter, home-style recipe. It is very easy to prepare and makes a wonderful late-night supper when you come home tired and think there is nothing in the house.

4 cups chicken broth
2 slices peeled fresh gingerroot (large pieces about 1 inch by ⅛ inch)
2 cloves garlic, peeled and smashed
1 teaspoon kosher salt
2 large eggs
1 teaspoon dry sherry
2 scallions, sliced, using all the white and most of the green
2 tablespoons chopped fresh cilantro

1. Bring the broth, gingerroot, and garlic to a boil. Lower the heat and simmer gently for 5 minutes. Discard the gingerroot and garlic. Stir in the salt. Lower the heat to a very low simmer.
2. In a small bowl, mix the eggs and sherry with a fork. Pour the eggs into the soup in a slow, steady stream, swirling them into the soup. The eggs will set in strands.
3. Remove from the heat and stir in the scallions and cilantro. Serve immediately.

Yield: 4 servings

Honey Noodle Kugel

Honey noodle kugel is sweet enough for dessert but is traditionally served at festive holiday meals as an accompaniment to a meat course, such as brisket or roasted chicken. It's ideal on a family reunion buffet because parents and kids love it equally. It can be served hot, but it can also be offered at room temperature. It cuts into tidy squares that small children like to take right off the serving platter.

8 ounces wide egg noodles
8 ounces reduced-fat or regular cream cheese, at room temperature
1 cup reduced-fat or regular sour cream
$1/2$ cup clover honey
4 large eggs
$1/2$ teaspoon kosher salt
$1/8$ teaspoon ground cinnamon

1. Cook the noodles in a large pot of boiling salted water until they are pliable but not soft, about 7 minutes. Drain and rinse.
2. Preheat the oven to 350 degrees. Coat a 9- by 13-inch baking dish with non-stick cooking spray. (Or use a $2^1/2$-quart oblong baking casserole and add 10 minutes to the baking time.)
3. Using an electric mixer, beat the cream cheese and sour cream together until smooth. Pour in the honey and beat until combined.
4. Add the eggs, 1 at a time, beating after each addition. Stir in the salt.
5. Stir the noodles into the batter so that they are well coated. Break apart any clumps of cooked noodles.
6. Spread in the baking pan and dust with cinnamon.
7. Bake for 30 to 35 minutes, until the kugel sets into a soft custard and the top is golden but not browned.

Yield: 10 servings

Spanish Garlic Soup

This soup has the big flavors and full body that are perfect for a winter dinner. It is finished in the oven like French onion soup, but in this case, instead of melted cheese, there is an egg poached on the surface.

3 tablespoons olive oil	4 cups chicken broth
6 cloves garlic, sliced	½ to 1 teaspoon kosher salt
1 teaspoon sweet paprika	Freshly ground pepper to taste
½ teaspoon ground cumin	4 large eggs
⅛ teaspoon ground saffron	2 tablespoons chopped fresh
4 thick slices crusty French bread	cilantro or parsley for garnish

1. Heat the olive oil in a heavy-bottomed pot. Add the garlic and cook over low heat about 10 minutes, until the garlic is soft and golden. Take care not to let it scorch or turn dark brown. Properly cooked, garlic becomes sweet and pungent but loses its sharpness.
2. Stir in the paprika, cumin, and saffron. Heat for 1 minute, until the aromas intensify.
3. Place the bread in the seasoned oil and toast on both sides.
4. Pour in the broth. Season with salt and pepper. Bring the broth to a boil and immediately lower the heat to a low simmer. If the soup boils too rapidly, the bread will break apart. That won't ruin it, but it looks much nicer with whole slices. Simmer for 20 minutes. Taste and add more salt if necessary (the saltiness of broth varies).
5. Preheat the oven to 400 degrees. Put 4 ovenproof soup bowls on a baking sheet. Ladle the soup and a slice of bread into each bowl. Crack an egg into each soup bowl. Slide the baking sheet into the oven (it's much easier than handling each bowl). Bake until the yolks are set, about 8 to 10 minutes. Garnish each bowl with cilantro or parsley.

Yield: 4 servings

Dessert Eggs

The simple egg is transformed in these dessert recipes, and it sometimes seems to me as magical as if the cook were a fairy godmother waving a wand over a pumpkin to make it into a jeweled coach. I love watching egg whites whip into a shiny high cloud of meringue. I love stirring egg yolks over heat and seeing them turn into a rich custard. And I love making the batter for biscotti, which is held together by eggs since there is no added fat. At the beginning of summer when all the hens are laying every day, the quantity of eggs gives me an excuse to make desserts. That makes everybody happy.

Angel Food Cake with Raspberry Sauce

If you've only tasted angel food cake purchased from a supermarket, this recipe will be a revelation. Unlike commercial angel food cakes, which often taste metallic and too sweet, this one has a clean flavor. Pour on the raspberry sauce, and you have a gorgeous finale to any meal.

When a recipe calls for this many egg whites, I measure out the volume instead of counting eggs. Egg size depends on who is laying and the time of year (the first eggs of spring are smaller). If I specified a number of "large eggs," I could be off by $\frac{1}{4}$ cup of white, which would make a huge difference in this cake. (See pages 5–6 for more about egg sizes and volume measurements.)

For the cake:
$1\frac{1}{4}$ cups egg whites (about 8 to 10 eggs)
$\frac{1}{2}$ teaspoon cream of tartar
$\frac{1}{4}$ teaspoon kosher salt
1 teaspoon vanilla extract
1 cup sugar
1 cup sifted cake or pastry flour

For the raspberry sauce:
2 cups frozen raspberries
$\frac{1}{4}$ cup light brown sugar
2 teaspoons raspberry liqueur
1 pint fresh raspberries

1. Put the rack in the bottom third of the oven and preheat the oven to 325 degrees. Get out a 10-inch angel food cake pan. Do not grease it.
2. In a large, clean, dry bowl, beat the egg whites and cream of tartar until soft peaks form. Add the salt and vanilla extract. (This is easiest to do in a stand mixer, but a handheld electric beater can be used. The whites will greatly increase in volume, so use the largest bowl you have.)
3. With the mixer running at full speed, add the sugar in a slow, steady stream. Beat until stiff, shiny peaks form. (The tips of the peaks will remain upright and not fall over.)

4. This is one of the few recipes where I sift the flour before measuring. It is very important that you have exactly the right amount of flour and that it is fluffy and free of lumps. Fold $\frac{1}{4}$ cup of flour into the egg whites. Continue to add small amounts of flour until all of it has been added and distributed evenly throughout the batter.

5. Spoon the mixture into the cake pan. Using a rubber spatula, smooth out the surface.

6. Bake for 35 to 40 minutes, until a toothpick inserted in the center of the cake comes out clean.

7. Put the cake pan upside down on a drying rack and let cool completely.

8. Meanwhile, make the raspberry sauce. Put the frozen raspberries, brown sugar, and liqueur in a small saucepan over low heat until the raspberries soften and burst. (Don't microwave.)

9. Strain the sauce through a fine-meshed sieve. Discard the seeds.

10. When the cake is cool, take a flexible spatula and run it along the sides of the pan to release the cake. Put the cake on a serving plate. Pour the sauce slowly over the top. Let some drip over the sides. Garnish with the fresh berries. Slice with a serrated knife or an angel food cake cutter.

Yield: 10 servings

Cocoa Angel Food Cake with Chocolate Espresso Glaze

This cake has a hint of cinnamon. The glaze is smooth, luscious, and dark in contrast to the airy texture of the cake. All in all, it is a lovely combination.

For the cake:
3/4 cup sifted pastry or cake flour
1/4 cup unsweetened cocoa powder
1/4 teaspoon kosher salt
1/2 teaspoon ground cinnamon
11/4 cups egg whites (about 8 to 10 eggs)
1/2 teaspoon cream of tartar
1 teaspoon vanilla extract
1 cup sugar

For the glaze:
6 ounces dark chocolate
2/3 cup heavy cream
3 tablespoons light corn syrup
1/4 teaspoon ground cinnamon
1/2 teaspoon instant espresso powder

1. Put the rack in the bottom third of the oven and preheat the oven to 325 degrees. Get out a 10-inch angel food cake pan.

2. Put the flour in a bowl. Sift in the cocoa powder, salt, and cinnamon. Stir until the ingredients are a uniform color.

3. In a large, clean, dry bowl, beat the egg whites and cream of tartar until foamy. Add the vanilla extract.

4. With the mixer running at full speed, add the sugar in a slow, steady stream.

Beat until stiff, shiny peaks form. (The tips of the peaks will remain upright and not fall over.)

5. Fold $1/4$ cup of the flour and cocoa mixture into the egg whites. Continue to add small amounts until all is blended into the batter. Fold gently.

6. Spoon the mixture into the cake pan. Using a rubber spatula, smooth the surface.

7. Bake for 35 to 40 minutes, until a toothpick inserted in the center of the cake comes out clean.

8. Put the cake pan upside down on a drying rack and let cool completely.

9. Meanwhile, make the glaze: Chop the chocolate into small pieces so that it melts evenly. Place the chocolate and the other ingredients in a small pot and heat gently until the chocolate melts. Stir frequently. Bring to a simmer and then immediately remove from the heat. Let it come to room temperature.

10. When the cake is cool, take a flexible spatula and run it along the sides of the pan to release the cake. Put the cake on a serving plate. Pour the sauce slowly over the top and sides. Use a spatula to even it out and coat all of the cake with the glaze. Slice with a serrated knife.

Yield: 10 servings

Orange and Almond Pound Cake

This is a classic pound cake in that eggs are the only leavener. As you beat the eggs into the batter, they create lift and the perfect crumb. I buy sliced almonds with the skins on, but you can use peeled almonds, too, or leave off the glaze and the nuts; that's how my sons like it. Either way, with or without nuts or glaze, the cake looks beautiful and tastes just the way a pound cake should.

For the cake:
½ pound (2 sticks) unsalted butter, at room temperature
3 cups sugar
6 large eggs
3 cups all-purpose flour, sifted before measuring
1 cup sour cream (not low-fat)
1 teaspoon vanilla extract
1 teaspoon almond extract
2 teaspoons grated orange zest

For the glaze:
1 cup confectioners' sugar
1 tablespoon orange juice, strained of any pulp
1 tablespoon hot water
3 tablespoons sliced almonds, toasted

1. Preheat the oven to 350 degrees. Coat a 10- to 12-cup Bundt pan with non-stick cooking spray.
2. Using an electric mixer, beat the butter with the sugar until the texture is fluffy.
3. Add the eggs to the mixing bowl 1 at a time, beating thoroughly after each addition.

4. Add one-third of the flour to the mixing bowl and beat. Add one-third of the sour cream. Beat. Continue in this way until all the flour and sour cream has been smoothly combined in the batter.

5. Stir in the vanilla and almond extracts and the orange zest. Note that one orange yields about 1 tablespoon of grated orange zest, which is the finely grated outer orange peel. Avoid using the white pith beneath, which is bitter. Once the zest is removed, squeeze the juice out of the orange and reserve it for the glaze.

6. Pour the batter into the Bundt pan and place it in the center of the oven. Bake about 1 hour, or until a toothpick comes out clean.

7. Let the cake cool in the pan on a wire rack. Remove the cake from the pan and place it on a sheet of aluminum foil.

8. To make the glaze: Using an electric mixer, beat the confectioners' sugar, orange juice, and hot water until the glaze is shiny and smooth. Immediately pour this glaze over the cake and let it drip down the sides. Dust with the almonds, which will stick to the glaze. When the glaze is set, place the cake on a serving plate.

Yield: 12 servings

All-Purpose Pastry Crust

All-butter pastry crusts taste wonderful, but they are softer and not as flaky as those made with solid shortening. I used to shy away from shortening because of the off-flavor and the trans fats. Now, however, you can buy solid shortening without hydrogenated fats. You can even find an organic version. If you want, you can also make this with all butter. Use 1 1/2 sticks of butter and no shortening. The rest of the recipe remains the same.

> 5 to 6 tablespoons ice water
> 1/4 pound (1 stick) unsalted butter, frozen
> 2 cups all-purpose flour
> 1/2 teaspoon kosher salt
> 1/3 cup solid shortening, chilled or frozen

1. This crust is made in a food processor fitted with the steel blade. The trick to a perfect crust is to use the pulse button. Never let the machine run more than about 3 seconds at a time. Also, start with frozen butter. If you plan ahead, measure out and freeze the shortening as well. Using a chef's knife, cut the frozen butter in half lengthwise, then slice it into 1/2-inch pieces. Have a measuring cup with ice water ready.

2. Put the flour, salt, and butter in the processor bowl. Pulse until all is crumbly. Add the solid shortening. Pulse briefly until the fats are in small pieces and evenly distributed throughout the flour.

3. Add the water, 1 tablespoon at a time, pulsing the machine in 3-second bursts after each addition. The dough should start to ball up. At this point remove it from the machine.

4. Pat the dough into a solid ball. Divide it in half and shape each half into a flattened round. Wrap tightly with plastic wrap and refrigerate for at least 30 minutes before rolling it out. The dough can be frozen, wrapped in plastic and then in aluminum foil, for up to 2 months. If frozen, thaw overnight in the refrigerator before using.

5. To roll it out, dust your countertop with flour. Using a rolling pin, push down on the dough, starting at the center and using outward strokes, lifting and turning the dough after every few pushes to make sure it doesn't stick and to keep it even all around.

6. When the dough is about 11 inches in diameter, fold it in half and then in half again so that it looks like a quarter of a pie. Place this in the pie plate and unfold. Trim off the ragged excess so that about 1 inch overhangs the edge of the pie plate. Tuck the overhanging dough under itself all the way around the edge so it just extends past the edge. Next, flute or press with a fork to decorate the edges.

7. If prebaking is called for, preheat the oven to 375 degrees. Place a piece of nonstick aluminum foil on the crust, loosely covering the edges of the pie. Weight down with pie weights or dry uncooked beans. Bake until golden and the edges begin to brown, about 12 to 15 minutes.

Yield: 2 single crusts for 9- to 10-inch pie plates

Graham Cracker Crust

Those store-bought graham cracker crusts look convenient, but not only are they in small, shallow pie tins, they don't taste half as good as this homemade version. This crust takes only a couple of minutes to make and is well worth the effort.

> **10 large (4½ by 2¼ inches) graham crackers**
> **2 tablespoons brown sugar**
> **6 tablespoons unsalted butter, melted**

1. Use a food processor to turn the crackers into crumbs. You will get about 1¼ cups of finely ground crumbs.
2. Add the brown sugar and pulse the machine. Add the butter and pulse until the mixture looks like wet sand. Do not let the machine run.
3. Turn out the crumb mixture onto a 9- or 10-inch pie plate. Press the mixture along the bottom and up the sides to make a firm and even crust.
4. If called for, prebake the crust in a preheated 350-degree oven for 10 minutes. The crust can be made a day ahead of time.

Yield: one 9- to 10-inch crust

Lemon Tart

Really good eggs do more than just thicken the tart: They provide a flavor base that mellows and blends the intense tartness of the lemons with the pure sweetness of the sugar. Unlike a custard pie recipe that requires a watchful eye and careful timing, all these ingredients need is a quick whisk in a bowl.

This lemon tart can be prepared in a 10-inch tart pan (shallow, with a removable bottom) or in a 9-inch pie plate. Top with a meringue (see page 106) or nothing at all.

1 All-Purpose Pastry Crust (page 100) or Graham Cracker Crust (page 102)
3 large eggs
3 egg yolks
½ cup lemon juice
1 cup sugar
½ cup heavy whipping cream
1 teaspoon grated lemon zest

1. Partially prebake the pastry according to the directions. Bake until it is only lightly golden because the crust will brown while the lemon filling bakes and then will bake further if a meringue is used. Prebaking is essential! I once tried to skip this step and the crust floated up to the surface and set there as the pie baked.
2. Preheat the oven to 375 degrees.
3. Whisk the ingredients together in the order listed. Whisk after each addition so that the batter is thoroughly blended though not bubbly.
4. Pour the filling into the pie plate and bake for 25 to 30 minutes, until set and slightly golden on the surface.

Yield: 8 servings

Peach Lemon Chiffon Pie

During peach season, it is worth it to peel and slice fresh, juicy peaches. But this essence of summer dessert can be made anytime of the year now that frozen peach slices are available in the supermarket.

1 Graham Cracker Crust (page 102)
2 cups peeled and sliced peaches, defrosted if frozen
1 envelope (1 tablespoon) unflavored gelatin
¼ cup water
4 large eggs, separated
1 cup sugar, divided
¼ cup fresh lemon juice
1 teaspoon grated lemon zest
¼ teaspoon kosher salt

1. Make the crust in a 9- or 10-inch deep pie plate and prebake according to the recipe. Set aside to cool.
2. Puree the peach slices. Measure out 1 cup of puree for this recipe.
3. Sprinkle the gelatin over the water and let soften for a few minutes.
4. In a small, heavy saucepan, whisk the egg yolks and 3/4 cup of the sugar. Place over medium heat and whisk constantly until foamy and hot but not boiling. Stir in the gelatin and water. Whisk for 30 seconds and then remove from the heat. Scrape into a bowl.
5. Stir the peach puree, lemon juice, and zest into the egg yolk mixture. Refrigerate for about 1½ hours, stirring occasionally, until it becomes the consistency of thick applesauce.
6. With an electric mixer, beat the egg whites and salt until soft peaks form. With the mixer running, slowly add the remaining ¼ cup of sugar. Beat until stiff.
7. Gently stir ½ cup of the peach mixture into the egg whites. Then fold the whites into the bowl with the peach mixture until combined.
8. Mound the filling into the piecrust. Chill for several hours before serving.

Yield: 8 servings

Chocolate Cream Pie with Meringue Topping

This pie should be made with the best dark chocolate you can find. The basic baker's chocolate at the supermarket won't do. It's worth making a special trip to get high-quality chocolate. Use a chocolate between 68 and 78 percent cacao for this.

For a cloud of sweetness on top of your pie, make a meringue topping. Not only will it put the perfect finish on the pie, but it will also use up those extra egg whites.

A true meringue topping for pie is delicate and ethereal. The whites whip up to glossy peaks, but within a few hours will weep out liquid and begin to collapse. Sure, this doesn't happen to "non-dairy whipped topping," and those mile-high pies at chain restaurants have stabilizers and other chemicals to keep them aloft, but, trust me, you want the real thing.

For the chocolate cream pie:
1 Graham Cracker Crust (page 102)
8 ounces dark chocolate, broken into small pieces
1 tablespoon unsalted butter, melted
1 teaspoon vanilla extract
^{2}/$_3$ cup sugar
^{1}/$_4$ cup cornstarch
^{1}/$_4$ teaspoon kosher salt
6 egg yolks
3 cups whole milk

For the meringue topping:
^{2}/$_3$ cup egg whites (between 4 to 6 whites)
^{1}/$_2$ cup sugar
^{1}/$_2$ teaspoon cream of tartar
^{1}/$_2$ teaspoon vanilla extract

1. Prepare the crust in a 9-inch deep pie plate. Prebake according to the directions in the recipe.
2. Melt the chocolate and butter in a bowl set over simmering water. Stir in the vanilla and set aside.
3. In a medium-sized heavy saucepan, whisk together the sugar, cornstarch, salt, and egg yolks. In a slow, steady stream, add the milk and whisk until well combined.
4. Over medium-high heat, bring the contents to a boil, whisking constantly. Once boiling, time for exactly 1 minute, whisking continually as it thickens. Remove from the heat.
5. Pour this sugar mixture into a fine-meshed sieve and push it through into the bowl with the chocolate. Stir to combine with the chocolate. Cover the surface with plastic wrap, place in the refrigerator, and cool completely, about 2 hours.
6. Scrape the filling into the piecrust, cover loosely, and chill at least 6 hours before serving. Top with the meringue or homemade whipped cream.
7. If you are going to top a pie with the meringue, preheat the oven to 375 degrees.
8. Place the whites and sugar in a heatproof bowl and set over a pot of hot (not boiling) water. Stir gently until the sugar dissolves. Remove from the pot and stir in the cream of tartar.
9. Using an electric mixer, beat the egg white mixture on high speed until high, stiff, and shiny. Stir in the vanilla extract.
10. Spread the meringue over the pie filling, making sure it touches the crust (to prevent shrinkage). Place in the oven about 4 inches from the top heating element.
11. Bake for 8 to 12 minutes, until the peaks of the meringue brown lightly.

Yield: 8 servings

Cranberry-Nut Tart

You usually don't think about eggs when you think about pecan pie, but without eggs the corn syrup and brown sugar would harden into an inedible mass. I'm not a big fan of pecan pie; to my taste it is usually cloyingly sugary. This dessert solves the problem by including fresh cranberries. Each mouthful is both tart and sweet. I've also used three types of nuts, which gives this tart a complexity of flavor and texture.

1 All-Purpose Pastry Crust (page 100)

3 large eggs

1 cup light brown sugar

½ cup light corn syrup

2 tablespoons unsalted butter, melted and cooled to room temperature

½ teaspoon kosher salt

1 tablespoon orange liqueur, such as Grand Marnier

1 cup fresh or frozen whole cranberries

½ cup walnuts, whole or halves

½ cup pecans, whole or halves

¼ cup cashews, whole or halves

1. Follow the directions for making the crust. Use a 10-inch tart pan (with a removable bottom) or a regular (not deep-dish) pie plate. Prebake according to the directions, until lightly golden brown.

2. Meanwhile, using a whisk, combine the eggs, brown sugar, corn syrup, butter, and salt. When smoothly blended, whisk in the orange liqueur.

3. Wash and pick through the cranberries. Discard any squishy or discolored berries. Stir into the batter. Stir in the nuts. Pour the filling into the tart pan, slide it onto a baking sheet, and put into the oven. Bake for 40 to 45 minutes, until the tart sets. If made in a pie plate, it will take longer to firm up. Let cool before removing from the tart pan.

Yield: 10 servings

Chocolate Kahlua Volcanoes

These "volcanoes" are the sort of an impressive, absolutely delicious dessert that causes conversation to stop as guests taste their first spoonful. Like soufflés, they rise and fall and are best eaten as soon as they come out of the oven, but as leftovers, collapsed and dense, they are still wonderful.

> 2 teaspoons sugar for dusting ramekins
> 4 ounces dark chocolate, broken into 1-ounce or smaller pieces
> ½ cup whipping cream
> 1 tablespoon Kahlua
> 4 egg whites
> 2 tablespoons sugar

1. Preheat the oven to 400 degrees. Butter four 6- or 8-ounce ramekins. Dust each one with sugar. Set on a baking sheet.
2. Warm (do not boil) the chocolate and cream in the microwave or in a small saucepan. Heat until the chocolate melts and the mixture begins to thicken. Stir in the Kahlua, then let cool. Set aside ⅓ cup.
3. Whip the egg whites on high until foamy. Keep beating while you gradually add the sugar. Continue to whip on high speed until the egg whites become stiff.
4. Take a big dollop from the main bowl of the chocolate mixture and fold it into the egg whites. Continue to add the chocolate, folding it gently into the egg whites until all but the reserved ⅓ cup has been combined with the egg whites. Spoon this egg white mixture into the ramekins.
5. Take the reserved ⅓ cup of chocolate and divide it evenly among the 4 ramekins, putting a large spoonful on top in the center of each one.
6. Bake about 12 minutes, until puffed and set.

Yield: 4 servings

Pumpkin Cheesecake

There are many styles of cheesecake. This one is creamy and, of course, rich.

1 Graham Cracker Crust (page 102)
Four 8-ounce packages cream cheese, softened
1 cup sugar
½ cup light brown sugar
½ cup sour cream
1 teaspoon vanilla extract
6 large eggs
¼ cup pumpkin puree
½ teaspoon ground ginger

1. Preheat the oven to 325 degrees. Coat a 10-inch springform pan with non-stick cooking spray. Line the bottom with a circle of parchment paper.
2. Press the graham cracker crust into the bottom of the springform pan. Bake for 12 minutes. Remove from the oven and let cool.
3. The cream cheese must be soft and at room temperature for this to come out smooth and creamy. Using an electric mixer, beat the cream cheese and sugars. Add the sour cream and beat until well mixed. Beat in the vanilla extract and eggs until smooth.
4. Scoop out 1¼ cups of the cheesecake filling and stir it into a bowl with the pumpkin puree and ground ginger.
5. Pour the plain cheesecake batter into the springform pan. Pour the pumpkin mixture into the center.
6. Take a knife and pull it through the cheesecake, as if slicing the batter into wedges. Then pull the knife through the batter in concentric circles.
7. Bake the cake in the center of the oven for 1 hour and 20 minutes, or until the center sets.

Yield: 10 servings

Chocolate Soufflé

Two of my favorite ingredients—eggs and chocolate—combine in this recipe to create a perfect dessert. Made with unsweetened chocolate, this recipe is an intense chocolate experience. But you can use milder, semisweet chocolate if preferred.

2 ounces unsweetened chocolate, broken into pieces
6 tablespoons sugar, divided, plus 1 teaspoon for dusting the dish
1 tablespoon water
2 tablespoons unsalted butter
⅛ teaspoon kosher salt
2 tablespoons all-purpose flour
¾ cup whole milk
3 large eggs, separated
1 teaspoon vanilla extract

1. Preheat the oven to 325 degrees. Butter a 1½-quart soufflé dish and dust with 1 teaspoon of sugar.
2. Combine the chocolate, 3 tablespoons of sugar, and the water in a small saucepan. Melt the chocolate over very low heat, stirring frequently until smooth. Set aside.
3. Melt the butter in a small pot. Stir in the salt and flour, and whisk constantly for 1 minute. Slowly pour in the milk and continue to whisk. Bring to a boil, then immediately lower the heat to a gentle simmer and whisk for 2 minutes, until thickened. Remove the pot from the heat and scrape the contents into a bowl.
4. Put the chocolate mixture into the bowl with the milk. Stir until well blended.
5. In a separate bowl, whisk the egg yolks until smooth. Scoop a little of the hot chocolate mixture into the bowl with the yolks and blend. Then stir all the yolks into the chocolate mixture. Stir in the vanilla extract.

6. Using an electric mixer, beat the egg whites until foamy. Add the remaining 3 tablespoons of sugar and beat until stiff.

7. Put one-third of the whites into the bowl with the chocolate and stir until combined. Take one-fourth of the chocolate mixture and stir it into the egg whites. Continue to add large dollops of egg whites until they are all folded into the chocolate.

8. Spoon the batter into the soufflé dish. Bake in the center of the oven for 30 to 35 minutes, until the soufflé has risen and is only a bit wobbly in the center when the dish is jiggled.

Yield: 4 servings

Chocolate Bread Pudding

I've made this with several types of bread, from hearty white bread, to challah, to Portuguese sweet bread. The challah makes a firm pudding. The Portuguese bread is soft and light, so the bread almost disappears into the pudding. As long as a quality home-style loaf of bread is used, the pudding will be good.

The size and shape of the casserole matters. A round and deep casserole will produce a pudding that is soft and gooey in the center. An oblong casserole will produce a pudding that is firmer throughout. This pudding can also be baked in individual portions in 6-ounce ramekins.

One 1-pound loaf white bread, unsliced
3 cups milk (1% or richer)
$\frac{1}{2}$ cup sugar
$\frac{1}{4}$ teaspoon kosher salt
8 ounces dark chocolate, broken into pieces
1 teaspoon vanilla extract
6 large eggs
$\frac{1}{2}$ cup bittersweet chocolate chips

1. Cut the bread into cubes. Coat a 3-quart baking dish with nonstick cooking spray.
2. Combine the milk, sugar, and salt in a medium saucepan. Whisk over medium heat until the sugar dissolves. Increase the heat and bring almost to a simmer. Remove from the heat and stir in the chocolate. Continue to stir gently until the chocolate has melted and the mixture is smooth. Stir in the vanilla extract.
3. In another bowl, whisk the eggs. When the chocolate mixture is lukewarm, slowly pour the eggs into the pot, stirring with a whisk until combined.
4. Put the bread cubes in the casserole. Pour the chocolate-egg mixture over the bread and press down on the bread so that it sinks into the batter. Dis-

tribute the chocolate chips on top. Cover tightly and refrigerate for a few hours or up to a day. This gives the bread time to absorb all of the batter evenly.

5. Pour 1 inch of water into a large pan and set it in the oven. (I like to use a roasting pan because the handles make it easier to take out of the oven later.) Preheat the oven to 350 degrees. While the oven is preheating, allow the bread pudding to come to room temperature on the kitchen counter.

6. Place the casserole in the hot water bath and bake, uncovered, for 50 minutes to 1 hour, until the pudding is set but still soft. For ramekins, reduce the baking time by about 20 minutes.

Yield: 10 servings

Ginger Pots de Crème

Like other recipes that use farmstead eggs, this one had to be adjusted. In a first test, using standard proportions for this classic French dessert, the farmstead yolks masked the delicate flavor of the gingerroot. I adjusted the recipe, using more fresh gingerroot and adding crystallized ginger. One other trick is to use salt to enhance flavor. The end result is a smooth, flavorful custard.

> One 2-inch piece fresh gingerroot
> 1 cup heavy cream
> 1½ cups whole milk
> 1 tablespoon minced crystallized ginger
> 2 egg yolks
> 2 large eggs
> ⅓ cup sugar
> ¼ teaspoon kosher salt
> 6 small pieces crystallized ginger for garnish

1. Peel the gingerroot and slice it thinly. Put it in a pot with the cream and milk. Bring to a boil and immediately turn off the heat. Pour it into a bowl. Let it rest for at least 30 minutes as the ginger steeps. Cool to room temperature.
2. Preheat the oven to 300 degrees. Put six 6- to 8-ounce ramekins in a baking dish. (I use a roasting pan because the handles make it safe to move from oven to counter.) Distribute the minced crystallized ginger evenly among the ramekins.
3. In a medium-sized bowl, whisk the yolks, eggs, sugar, and salt. Pour the milk mixture into the eggs. Gently whisk (don't make bubbles) until combined. Strain this mixture through a fine-meshed sieve into a lipped measuring cup or bowl. Discard the ginger. Pour the mixture into the ramekins.
4. Place the baking dish in the oven. Pour hot water around the ramekins until it

comes halfway up their sides. The water bath gives the custard a soft texture. If you start with cold water, they will take longer to bake.

5. Bake for 30 to 40 minutes, until the custards are set but slightly wobbly in their centers. Take the baking dish out of the oven and carefully remove the ramekins from the water bath. Place a piece of crystallized ginger on top of each ramekin. Cool on a wire rack, cover with plastic wrap, and refrigerate. These will keep for 2 days.

Yield: 6 pots de crème

Chocolate Walnut Meringue Cookies

This is my favorite way to use up extra egg whites.

> 4 ounces dark chocolate
> 3 egg whites
> $\frac{1}{8}$ teaspoon cream of tartar
> $\frac{3}{4}$ cup sugar, divided
> 4 ounces (1 cup) finely chopped walnuts

1. Preheat the oven to 300 degrees. Line 2 baking sheets with parchment paper.
2. Break the chocolate into small pieces and melt it in the microwave, using low power. Stir and let cool.
3. Using a stand mixer or handheld electric mixer, beat the egg whites and cream of tartar until soft peaks form. While the machine is running, add $\frac{1}{2}$ cup of sugar, 1 tablespoon at a time. Beat until shiny and very stiff peaks form.
4. Using a spatula, fold in the remaining sugar and then the chocolate. Stir gently. You don't have to mix it perfectly; thin streaks of egg whites and chocolate can remain. Stir in the walnuts until distributed throughout.
5. Using 2 teaspoons, drop large dollops of meringue onto the cookie sheets, spacing them about 3 inches apart.
6. Bake for 20 to 25 minutes. If baking on two oven shelves, switch the cookie sheets and rotate them. Bake until the cookies form a light, dry exterior but have a slightly chewy center.

Yield: 18 to 20 cookies

Pistachio Apricot Biscotti

The deep-yellow color of the egg yolks comes through in the batter, and the green pistachios and orange apricots make colorful highlights.

1 cup shelled raw pistachios
3 cups all-purpose flour
1½ cups sugar
¼ teaspoon kosher salt
1 teaspoon baking powder

¾ cup coarsely chopped dried
  apricots
5 large eggs
1 teaspoon vanilla extract

1. Preheat the oven to 300 degrees. Line 2 cookie sheets with parchment paper.
2. Put the pistachios on a rimmed baking sheet and toast in the oven about 10 minutes, or until they begin to change color but not darken. Set aside to cool.
3. In a large bowl, stir together the flour, sugar, salt, and baking powder. Using your fingers, separate the sticky chopped apricots and toss them in the flour until the apricots are evenly mixed throughout. Stir in the pistachios.
4. In a small bowl, whisk the eggs and vanilla extract until no streaks of egg whites remain. Stir this into the flour mixture. The dough will be very sticky.
5. Flour your hands and knead the dough so that it forms a rough loaf shape.
6. Place the dough on one of the cookie sheets. Shape it into a rectangle about 13- by 4-inches in size. Bake for 50 minutes.
7. Remove the biscotti from the oven and let cool for 10 minutes. Then, using a serrated knife on a cutting board, cut it into slices ½-inch thick. Put the cookies, flat side down, on the cookie sheets. Bake for 20 minutes. Remove from the oven, flip the cookies over, and then bake 20 minutes more, until golden.
8. Place the cookies on drying racks to cool. Store in an airtight container for up to 2 weeks.

Yield: 16 cookies

Index